From A Speck of Dust
To A Son of God

Why Were You Born?

by
Fred R. Coulter

York Publishing Company
Post Office Box 1038
Hollister, California 95024-1038

Unless otherwise noted,
all Scriptures used in
this book are quoted from:
*The Holy Bible In Its
Original Order—A Faithful
Version With Commentary
ISBN 978-0-9819787-0-3*

Cover image: Henrik Jonsson - <u>henrikjonsson.com</u>

*ISBN 978-0-9961757-0-8
Copyright 2016
York Publishing Company
Post Office Box 1038
Hollister, California 95024-1038*

Table of Contents

About the Author .... *i*

Other Works by the Author .... *ii*

Other Key CBCG Publications .... *iv*

Acknowledgments .... *v*

Foreword .... *vi*

Introduction .... *viii*

CHAPTER ONE Do Men Know *Why* There Is Human Life? 1

CHAPTER TWO Where Do We Begin? 10

CHAPTER THREE Man and Woman Created in God's
　　　　Image and *Likeness* 16

CHAPTER FOUR God Continues to Create Through
　　　　Human Procreation 26

CHAPTER FIVE God's Covenant with Abraham 52

CHAPTER SIX The *Family* Nature of God 59

CHAPTER SEVEN Jesus Christ and the Redemption of
　　　　Man and Woman... 64

CHAPTER EIGHT What Jesus Christ Teaches About Eternal Life ... 74

CHAPTER NINE Why Are Many Called, But Few Chosen? 80

CHAPTER TEN Rescued from Satan the Devil
　　　　to Walk in Newness of Life 90

CHAPTER ELEVEN A Later Revelation: The Sonship of God 99

CHAPTER TWELVE The Ultimate Revelation of Jesus Christ—
　　　　From a Speck of Dust to a Son of God 114

CONCLUSION... 137

Epilogue 140

Appendix One Seven Proofs God Exists 141

Appendix Two Did God Create Satan the Devil? 146

Appendix Three What Happens After Death? 151

Appendix Four Does the Bible Teach the Trinity? 159

Appendix Five Can the Sin of Abortion Be Forgiven? 164

Appendix Six What Does it Mean to Be "Born Again" or
　　　　"Born of God"? 167

About the Author

Fred R. Coulter attended the University of San Francisco and graduated from San Mateo State College before graduating from Ambassador University (Ambassador College), Pasadena, California, with a BA in Theology in 1964. He was ordained a minister of Jesus Christ in 1965 and pastored churches of God in the Pacific Northwest, the Mountain States, the greater Los Angeles area, and Monterey, California, including the central coast area. Mr. Coulter completed advanced biblical and ministerial studies in 1972-75 under the Ambassador University Master's Program. While completing these studies, he was encouraged by his professor of *koiné* Greek, Dr. Charles V. Dorothy, to consider translating the books of the New Testament.

For the next twenty years, Mr. Coulter diligently studied, continuing to expand his knowledge of *koiné* Greek, being mentored and guided by Dr. Dorothy. While undertaking a verse-by-verse study of the Greek New Testament, he was moved to translate the New Testament into clear, easy-to-read English for contemporary readers—resulting in *The New Testament In Its Original Order* (now incorporated into *The Holy Bible In Its Original Order—A Faithful Version With Commentary*).

With a ministry now spanning over 50 years, Fred Coulter has dedicated his life and talents to *Restoring Original Christianity for Today*. Laying aside all traditions of men, he has preached and translated the *truth* of the Scriptures as taught by Jesus Christ and the apostles—proclaiming Jesus as personal Savior for all. Since 1983, Mr. Coulter has been the president of the Christian Biblical Church of God, headquartered in Hollister, California. He has an active ministry that reaches all parts of the United States and Canada, with hundreds of fellowship groups and numerous congregations. There are additional offices in Australia, New Zealand, the United Kingdom, South Africa, Ethiopia, Kenya, and Nigeria.

Each year over *two million* people from around the world actively utilize the church's Web sites where you will find timely, inspiring weekly messages—audio and video—and in-depth verse-by-verse biblical study materials covering virtually all of Scripture (**www.cbcg.org**, **www.churchathome.org** and **www.afaithfulversion.org**).

Other Works by the Author

The Holy Bible In Its Original Order—A Faithful Version With Commentary is a new translation that reflects the meaning of the original Hebrew and Greek with fidelity and accuracy—and is the only English version in a single volume in which the books of the Bible are arranged in their original manuscript order. This easy-to-read translation retains the grace and grandeur of the *King James Version* while resolving hundreds of its improperly translated passages. These passages have led countless theologians and believers to accept doctrines that are contrary to the true meaning of the New Testament Greek and Old Testament Hebrew.

Included are many commentaries on the writing, canonization, and preservation of the Scriptures, and various appendices cover numerous controversial teachings. Detailed footnotes and marginal references explain hard-to-understand passages. This version is a vital tool for all students of the Bible! See **www.theoriginalbiblerestored.com**. The complete Bible is available with downloadable text and audio presentation by Fred R. Coulter at **www.afaithfulversion.org**.

A Harmony of the Gospels in Modern English brings to life the message and purpose of the true Jesus, portraying His life and ministry in their true scriptural and historical settings—and it includes all the vital information missing from Bill O'Reilly's *Killing Jesus*. This easy-to-understand, step-by-step account of the life of Christ is an indispensable study aid for every Bible student.

The Christian Passover details the scriptural and historical truths of the Passover in both the Old and New Testaments, leading the reader step-by-step through every aspect of one of the most vital and fundamental teachings revealed in the Bible. With over 500 pages, the book fully explains the meaning of the Christian Passover—a remembrance of the sacrifice of Jesus Christ, the Passover Lamb of God—in a most compelling and inspiring manner. The full meaning of the body and blood of Jesus Christ is revealed, showing the magnitude of God's love for every person.

The Day Jesus the Christ Died—the Biblical Truth about His Passion, Crucifixion and Resurrection is the *only book* to present "the rest of the story"—left out by Mel Gibson in his epic movie "The Passion of the Christ." Without the true historical and biblical facts, one cannot fully understand the true meaning of Jesus Christ's horrific, humiliating, and gruesome death by beating, scourging, and crucifixion. The author presents the full biblical account in a most compelling way. As you will see, the truth is more astounding than all of the ideas, superstitions, and traditions of men!

The Seven General Epistles is designed for an in-depth verse-by-verse study of the epistles of James; I and II Peter; I, II and III John and Jude. As part of the living Word of God, these epistles are especially meaningful for personal Christian growth today—just as when they were originally written. It is impossible to understand *Original Christianity for Today* without fully understanding the writings of the apostles of Jesus Christ.

Occult Holidays or God's Holy Days—Which? For centuries the leaders of Orthodox Christendom have sold popular holidays—Halloween, Christmas, Easter, etc.—to the masses as though they had "Christian" meaning. This book effectively demonstrates that these celebrated holidays are *not* of God—never have been of God—but originated from ancient religions rooted in occultism. Contrary to the false ideas of men, the *true* biblical holy days of God have vital spiritual meaning and demonstrate God's fantastic plan of salvation for all mankind.

God's Plan for Mankind Revealed by His Sabbath and Holy Days. This first-of-its-kind, 598-page work provides a comprehensive look at God's amazing Master Plan for the human family—precisely as it is outlined by the biblical seventh-day Sabbath and annual holy days. Each chapter is a transcript of an in-depth message or Bible study revealing God's purpose from Genesis to Revelation. All the messages are included on an accompanying set of CDs. It is not possible to comprehend the complete Plan of God through Jesus Christ, called the *Mystery of God*, without the scriptural knowledge of God's weekly Sabbath and annual holy days.

Lord, What Should I Do? "Christianity" is now facing an unprecedented crisis: disenchanted churchgoers are quitting by the thousands, looking for genuine spirituality *outside* of the corporate church. This book presents *real solutions* to the problems of a dysfunctional "Christianity," emphasizing how Christians *can* and *must* take steps to recapture a faith that is authentic, relevant, and applicable to modern life—even if it means leaving organized "Christianity."

The Appointed Times of Jesus the Messiah. Mainstream Christianity has little or no understanding of how Jesus' messianic role has been carefully organized according to what Scripture calls God's "appointed times." As this book demonstrates, the "appointed times" of the Messiah follow the timeframe set by the biblical *festivals* and *holy days* as well as the *70-week prophecy* of Daniel nine—all of which outline God's plan of salvation. Indeed, it is only within this unique context that the role of Jesus as the Messiah can be rightly understood. This book also lays out the scriptural sequence of events leading to the powerful, awesome return of Jesus Christ to save the world from utter destruction!

In-Depth Bible Study Transcript Books. For the serious Bible student, the CBCG has developed over 50 books transcribed from audio messages or studies (each book includes an accompanying CD/CDs). These books cover essential Bible teachings in great detail, such as: *The Love of God, Grace of God in the Bible, Grace of God and Commandment Keeping, Grace Upon Grace, Keys to Answered Prayer, Daniel and Revelation Prophecy Series, Judge Righteous Judgment, Holy Sabbath, Romans Series, Hebrews Series, Gospel of John Series. Galatians Series, I Corinthians Series, Pastoral Series, Ephesians Series, Philippians Series, Colossians Series, God's Healing, Seven Church Harvest, Wealth and Income—Tithes and Offerings, Secret Rapture Hoax, How to Use God's Holy Spirit, Washing of the Water by the Word*, and many more.

Booklets and Online Studies. We also have additional written materials (numerous articles and over 30 booklets). These articles and booklets and all the transcript books are available in audio and video format, which can be downloaded at **www.cbcg.org**, **www.churchathome.org** and **www.afaithfulversion.org**.

Other Key CBCG Publications

Additional full-length books by other authors include:

Judaism—Revelation of Moses or Religion of Men? Contrary to Jewish claims, the religion of Judaism does *not* represent the way of life God gave through Moses in the Old Testament. In fact, Judaism greatly distorts the biblical Law of Moses by adding to it a massive humanly-devised "code" of laws. The result is that Jews can no longer differentiate between *God's Law* and man-made *tradition*. Using history, Scripture and the Jews' own writings, this book demonstrates that Judaism is actually a *false religion* developed by men.

America and Britain—Their Biblical Origin and Prophetic Destiny. The Bible mentions all the great ancient empires: Egypt, Assyria, Babylon, Medo-Persia, Greece, Rome. But what about the *greatest empire* in history, the British Empire? What about the most powerful nation in all of history, the United States? Their *apparent absence* from the Bible has long puzzled scholars. As this book shows, these great nations are, in fact, discussed in numerous passages of the Bible—where they are identified by their *ancient, ancestral names*. Utilizing Scripture and documented history, the author shows just who the British and American peoples *really are*—revealing both their biblical origin and astounding prophetic destiny.

Key booklets include: *God, or No God?, What the Bible Teaches About Clean and Unclean Meats, Are Enoch and Elijah in Heaven?*, and *Why is Christianity Failing in America?*

Acknowledgments

We first acknowledge God the Father and Jesus Christ, and thank them for preserving the Holy Bible—in spite of mankind's tumultuous history—so that today, God's truth is available for everyone. It is the very Word of God that gives us the true understanding of the purpose of human existence. Jesus said, "Your Word is the truth" (John 17:17), and "you shall know the truth, and the truth shall set you free" (John 8:32).

Primarily, I give my heartfelt gratitude and appreciation to my loving, dear wife, Dolores, for her personal encouragement and assistance. A special "thank you" goes to all the faithful brethren whose freewill tithes and offerings made this book possible. Through their spirit of giving, each one of them has a special part in helping to preach and spread the Gospel of Jesus Christ.

Special thanks goes to Randy Vild for his much-needed research. Thanks also to Philip Neal for his editing, and to John and Hiedi Vogele for their proofreading and final formatting of the text. As with my other publications, many people have helped and shared in the production of this book. Their diligent work and support has made it possible.

Foreword

In our hectic world, people rarely take the time to ask, let alone really ponder: *What is the meaning of life? Why am I here? What is the purpose of mankind?*

And for those who *do* ask, where can they turn for answers? Steeped in evolution, the world's universities don't know the answer—they only mock the question. Science, which relies solely on what can be seen and measured, can only offer a theory. Our political leaders, who are invested mostly in maintaining the status quo and winning the next election, don't have a clue.

Surely our religious leaders know—after all, it's their job. And if you ask, they'll tell you: "The purpose of human life is to get to one's eternal reward in heaven." But many find this answer to be all too nebulous. Could it be that we are missing something? Could it be that we have it all wrong?

According to Revelation 12, Satan the devil has the *whole world* in the grip of massive deceptions by fully appealing to the power of human self-delusion (verse 9). This includes every source of knowledge you can imagine: education, philosophy, science, even religion. Yes, *especially* religion. Why would Satan do this? Because he's *hiding* something from us—from you. He doesn't want you to know the *truth* about human existence, about mankind's purpose.

The renowned physicist Stephen Hawking once said, "The greatest enemy of knowledge is not ignorance, it is the *illusion* of knowledge." This is substantially true of all science, philosophy and religion. And quite frankly, today's "Christianity" in particular is predicated on the *illusion* of knowledge. Its leaders claim to have the answers to life's greatest mysteries—such as, *Why were you born?*—but only offer lip service to God as they pump up their biblically-illiterate followers with humanistic feel-good-ism. And the idea of going to heaven certainly makes people *feel* good. But is that really what the Bible teaches? Is there nothing of *greater substance* to human existence?

If you're like most people, you don't have the time or the inclination to really look into the matter. *Or do you?* Most of us are just too busy enjoying the pleasures of life. We chase after happiness by amassing physical, material *things*. We get caught up in our various routines and never stop long enough to ask the big questions. It's like Jesus warned, the "cares of this world" *choke out* anything truly spiritual. That's why this society has a carnival-like atmosphere, driven by the massive media/entertainment industry, producing a make-believe reality: Satan wants you fully distracted so you can't *think*—and can't ask the big questions.

But these days are full of stress and fear, conflict and evil, war and terror. For some, this makes them stop and think: Is mankind rushing head-long into oblivion? Where is all this heading? What happened to God? Why isn't He doing something?

Maybe He is and you just don't know it!

That's what this book is all about—removing the satanic blindness so you can *see* what God is really doing. So you can understand *why* God created mankind. So you can know *why you were born!*

Every living thing strives toward growth, endeavors unconsciously to fulfill its God-ordained potential. It's a law of nature. But not so for humans. Because man is a *thinking* creature with a god-like will, we live by the *choices* we make. And more often than not, those choices lead us into conflict with God's way of life. The inevitable results are unhappiness, suffering, destruction, and death. Indeed, we see it all around us.

But what if our choices were more deliberate—grounded on God's Word and in harmony with His grand design? Then we too would strive toward growth; we would *consciously* live to fulfill our human potential and eternal destiny—because we would know *why* we were born.

To be sure, there can be no more important knowledge than to understand the *purpose* for which you draw breath. *From a Speck of Dust to a Son of God—Why Were You Born?* peels back the layers of deception that have kept man and woman in the dark about this all-important knowledge of God. All the reader needs is his or her Bible and a mind that is open and willing to be taught—to be shown the marvelous eternal future God has planned for those who truly love Him.

Let this book be your guide—because God's purpose for your life is far greater than you have dared to imagine!

Fred R. Coulter

Introduction

Why were you born? *Where* did man come from? Is human life the end result of blind evolution, devoid of any purpose? Or, is human life a special creation of an all-powerful God? If someone were to ask you these questions, how would you answer?

What if there actually is a great, little-known purpose for human life? Wouldn't you want to know—to understand? *How* and *where* can we discover this ultimate secret, this mystery of the ages—the true purpose of human life—of YOUR LIFE?

It is a startling fact that *none* of the great philosophers, scientists, or religionists—ancient or contemporary—know *why* human life exists. In spite of their various theories, they are unable to demonstrate any overarching *purpose* for human life. Nor can they account for the reality that man and woman have such great potential—can do such marvelous things—yet possess a nature that is absolutely destructive and ends only in death. *Why* do they of all people not understand?

In their grossly misguided efforts to comprehend human existence, they have rejected the fact that there is a *Creator God* Who has sovereign rule over the heavens, the earth, and all life! They do not consider that God has revealed Himself to mankind *through* His creation, and that His inspired Word, the Bible, reveals His *purpose* for creating man. In spite of the fact that today there are billions of Bibles covering every major language, they arrogantly reject it. At the same time, they tenaciously cling to their empty faith in the theory of evolution and vain religions. Thus, by scornfully rejecting the Word of God, they dismiss the only source that can truly answer the question, *What is the all-encompassing purpose of human life?*

This book, *From a Speck of Dust to a Son of God—Why Were You Born?*, lays out in a step-by-step sequence the mind-boggling truth, from the Scriptures, of God's loving, incredible plan and purpose for your life.

An Overview of the "Mystery of God"

In the ages of eternity past, long before the foundation of the world, God devised a plan that would *expand* His Divine Family of immortal spirit beings. This plan is rooted in God's magnificent love—"For God is love!" (I John 4:8, 16); it is a reflection of His desire to *share* all that He is and all that He has. But *how* would God accomplish such an incredible feat?

The focal point of this plan was God's creation of man and woman. His love for them is clearly manifested by the fact that He said, "Let Us make man in Our image, after Our likeness.... And God created man in His *own* image, in the image of God He created him. He created them male and female" (Gen 1:26-27).

Imagine that—being created in God's *own* image!

The creation of Adam was unique and exceptional—for God personally formed him from the dust of the ground with His own hands and breathed into him the breath and spirit of life. Then, using one of Adams ribs, God formed the first woman, Eve—also a unique creation.

Adam and Eve were the pinnacle of God's physical creation, and He gave them the whole world as a gift. God blessed them and said, "Let them **have dominion** over the fish of the sea and over the fowl of heaven and over the livestock and **over all the earth** and over every creeping thing that crawls upon the earth.... **Be fruitful and multiply**, and **replenish the earth, and subdue it**..." (verses 26, 28). Two things stand out from this key passage: The aspect of having *dominion* over the earth is an early hint at mankind's awesome worldwide purpose; and the fact that God created humans as male and female—able to *reproduce* after their own God-image kind—hints at God's desire to expand His family!

So beautiful and wonderful was God's creation of the world—and of man and woman—that He "saw everything that He had made, and indeed, *it was exceedingly* good" (verse 31).

The Power of Human Free Moral Agency

God did not create mankind to be automatons or preprogramed, unthinking, mechanical robots. Rather, because of the wonderful godlike abilities He created *within* man and woman, He gave them *independent free moral agency*—the ability and obligation to choose and decide for themselves how they would live. This is why God gave them His laws and commandments—which, if they *chose* to obey, would lead to a blessed physical life. The *Tree of Life* in the middle of the Garden of Eden symbolized the way of God for mankind, which would lead to eternal life. But Adam and Eve would have to *choose* to believe God, to love Him, and to keep His laws and commandments.

God also placed in the Garden the *Tree of the Knowledge of Good and Evil*. But He strictly commanded them to *not* eat of this tree. He emphatically warned them that if they chose to eat of this tree, the result would be death—"in dying you shall surely die"! Thus, this tree symbolized the way of man and woman *choosing* to live in disobedience to their Creator God.

Would Adam and Eve use their free moral agency to *decide for themselves* what was good and what was evil, instead of believing God? If they chose to eat of the fruit of this forbidden tree, they would bring upon themselves and their descendants the corrective punishment of God because of their sins. Moreover, they would be *blinded* to the true purpose of human existence.

On the other hand, if Adam and Eve should *choose to love God* and obey Him, He would bless them beyond imagination. Moreover, God would have revealed to them His ultimate plan for their *eternal destiny*—including His plan for their progeny—all mankind!

But using cunning deception, the serpent, Satan the devil, persuaded Adam and Eve to eat of the fruit of the forbidden tree—claiming that "in dying they would *not* die." He promised that if they ate of this tree, they would become wise like God—able to *decide for themselves* what was good and what was evil. In the end, they chose to *not* rely on God; rather, they would exercise their free moral agency and trust their own judgment.

After Adam and Eve ate of the forbidden fruit, their eyes were indeed *opened*—because they had practiced and experienced evil! But tragically, their minds were *closed* and they became antagonistic toward God.

Their sin and rebellion against their Creator resulted first in God's judgment against the serpent—wherein God promised a future Redeemer who would destroy the works of the devil and give His life as a sacrifice for the sins of mankind (Gen. 3:15). In His judgment for Adam and Eve's sin, God placed over them the sentence of death—as He had warned, "In dying, you shall surely die." He then drove them from the Garden of Eden, denying them access to the *Tree of Life*. However, because it was vital to God's plan that they increase the human family through procreation, they did not die immediately but lived for over 900 years.

The Ultimate Destiny of Mankind
Became Hidden as the "Mystery of God"

When God promised a future Savior, He also purposely delayed revealing His plan for mankind until that "Anointed One" should come, which would be over 4,000 years later. Thus, God *hid* this knowledge from Adam and Eve and their descendants. This is why the Bible describes God's plan for mankind as the "mystery of God." From the time of Adam and Eve until Jesus Christ, God only revealed certain aspects of this profound mystery to the few faithful patriarchs, such as Enoch, Noah, Abraham, Isaac, and Jacob. Later, He revealed key knowledge to Moses—an important prophecy of the coming Messiah (Deut. 18:15-22). When David was king over Israel, God revealed through the book of Psalms quite a number of details concerning the yet future life, death, and resurrection of Jesus Christ—as well as His coming world-ruling kingdom. Likewise, scattered throughout the books of the prophets are numerous additional aspects of the coming Messiah and His kingdom.

When the appointed time came for Jesus, "God manifested in the flesh," to begin His prophesied ministry, He chose special men to train as His apostles. Importantly, He told them that they would be given special understanding of the mysteries of God that had never been revealed to mankind.

Jesus told them, "Because **it has been given to you to know the mysteries of the kingdom of heaven**…. [*Thus,*] blessed *are* your eyes, because they see; and your ears, because they hear. For truly I say to you, many prophets and righteous *men* have desired to see what you see, and have not seen; and to hear what you hear, and have not heard" (Matt. 13:11, 16-17).

As Jesus' earthly ministry was coming to a conclusion in 30 AD, He told His apostles that He had yet many things to reveal to them—but added that they were not able to handle such exceptional knowledge at that time. However, He promised that after He was raised from the dead, and had returned to heaven, He would begin to reveal *new understanding* to them through the power of the Holy Spirit (John 16:12-15).

Just as promised, in 52-56 AD, over two decades after His resurrection, Jesus began to reveal key aspects of the hidden "mystery of God"—beginning with the "sonship of God" (Gal. 4:5-6). Then, in 61-62 AD, the apostle Paul wrote that God had revealed to the apostles and prophets the *full* "mystery of God"—"**the mystery that has been hidden from ages and from generations**, but has now been revealed to His saints; to whom **God did will to make known what** *are* **the riches of the glory of this mystery**…" (Col. 1:26-27).

As found in the New Testament writings of His apostles, Jesus indeed gave them the full revelation of the secret "mystery of God"—the profound ultimate *destiny* of the "called, chosen, and faithful." This is the revelation of God the Father, through Jesus Christ, concerning His plan for you! It answers the ultimate question, *Why were you born?* It reveals your future— *from a speck of dust to a son of God!*

Do Men Know *Why*
There Is Human Life?

Man has discovered—by way of astronomy and related sciences—our own solar system, the Milky Way galaxy, and the awe-inspiring, infinite and incomprehensible universe beyond. Employing recently developed sophisticated technology, space telescopes and satellites, scientists have captured images not only of *our* galaxy, but have also documented the existence of *billions* of additional galaxies located in the furthest reaches of the universe.

Similarly, man has explored the depths of the oceans with deep-sea submarines. Using powerful microscopes, researchers have analyzed the makeup of living cells—even peered into the structure of atoms. Increasingly, scientists are astonished to realize that microstructures found on earth often mirror the various macrostructures of the universe. Yet they do not grasp the *significance* of such discoveries—that there is indeed a "grand design."

Scientists have also discovered the genetic processes by which almost all living plants and creatures, including humans, procreate. In fact, the study of the human body and mind—including man's unique ability to create, invent, and find expression through music, art and literature—continues as one of the great frontiers of scientific research.

To say that man is *preoccupied* with his own existence is an understatement. Indeed, of all living creatures, only man asks *why*. Yet *no* scientific discovery, conclusion or theory can begin to answer the basic question of human life: ***Why does man exist?***

Throughout the ages men have asked: *What is man? Why is there human life?* Is human life a product of "evolution," or a unique creation of God? What is the purpose for human life—for *your* life? Is it even possible to know? Where can we look for answers to this all-important question?

In search of answers, we will first look at what the great religions of the world tell us. As we will see, it is quite a bewildering hodgepodge of beliefs! Then we will examine the varied ideas of the "intellectual elite"—secularists, atheists, evolutionists, and philosophers. Have any of them, individually or collectively, actually discovered the true *purpose* for human life? Can they explain this greatest of mysteries—***Why were you born?***

Chapter One

What the Religions of this World Believe

Professing Christianity: Essentially, the Christian religion teaches that when one's life comes to an end, the person's "immortal soul" immediately goes to *heaven* or *hell*, depending on whether they have lived a good life or an evil life. (For Catholics, there is also the possible step of being sent to *purgatory*, a kind of in-between state, in order to have one's evil purged through priestly prayers.) For the "Christian," making it *into heaven* is presumably the supreme purpose for mankind. Yet that thoroughly unbiblical perspective, owing to its absolute ambiguity, fails to satisfactorily answer the question, *What is the purpose for human existence?*

Other Religions of the World: Because they reject the God of the Bible and His divine revelation, the key religions of the world also fail to identify the true purpose for human life. Consequently, they have created their own particular beliefs—disconnected from the Word of God. Here is a brief overview:[1]

Judaism: Traditional Judaism teaches that death is *not* the end of human existence. However, because Judaism is primarily focused on life here and now, the religion approaches the afterlife with little dogma. This leaves considerable room for personal opinion. Thus, many Orthodox Jews, like Christians, believe that the "souls" of the righteous go to "paradise" at death—or to a place similar to hell. Ideas resembling reincarnation are also held, as are views supporting a resurrection at the inauguration of the "messianic age." The Talmud teaches that this world is like a "corridor" leading to the *olam ha-ba*, the afterlife in the world to come. The goal of devout Jews is to live a life worthy of passing from the corridor into eternal paradise.

Buddhism: The purpose of life is to bring an end to one's suffering by gaining enlightenment, awakening and a release from the cycle of death and birth—or to at least attain a better rebirth by gaining merit. Our purpose is also to help others do the same.

Hare Krishna: Similar to Indian religions, the purpose of life focuses on reincarnation, which must continue until one is united with the godhead through "Krishna consciousness."

Hinduism: The purpose of life is to realize that we are even now part of God. With this understanding we can ultimately leave the earth and abide with God.

Jainism: The universe is eternal and many gods exist—and gods, humans, and all living things are classified in a complex hierarchy. The soul is uncreated and eternal and can attain perfect divinity. The purpose of life is to gain liberation from the cycle of death and rebirth. This is accomplished by avoiding bad karma, and especially by causing no harm to others.

Sikhism: The purpose of life is to overcome the self and align one's life with the will of God—thus becoming a saintly soldier, fighting for good. Reincarnation must continue until a person's karma is resolved and merged with God.

Stoicism: The purpose of life is happiness, which is achieved by virtue and living according to the dictates of reason, ethical and philosophical training, self-reflection, careful judgment, and an inner calm.

Taoism: The purpose of life is to achieve inner harmony, peace and longevity by living in accordance with Tao—the path or the way—and to ultimately revert back to a state of non-being, which is said to be the "other side of being."

Traditional Chinese Religion: Man's purpose is to live a favorable life and peaceful afterlife—attained through rituals, ancestor worship, prayer, longevity practices, divination, prophecy, astrology, and *feng shui* (a Chinese system of law).

Confucianism: Confucianism is as much a code of life for organizing the state as it is a religion or a philosophy. It recognizes that human nature must be shaped through discipline and education. Because man is driven by both positive and negative influences, Confucianists seek to achieve a goodly nature through strong relationships and careful reasoning while working to minimize negative energy. This emphasis on normal living is seen in the Confucianist scholar Tu Wei-Ming's statement that "we can realize the ultimate meaning of life in ordinary human existence." Thus, in Confucianism, the purpose of life is to fulfill one's role in society with propriety, honor and loyalty.

Islam: In Islam, man's ultimate objective is to serve Allah by abiding by the divine guidelines revealed in the *Qur'an* and in the tradition of the prophet Mohammad. Earthly life is merely a test, determining one's after-life, either in *Jannat* (paradise) or in *Jahannum* (hell).

Utilitarianism: Founded on the writings of Jeremy Bentham (1748-1832), Utilitarianism teaches that nature has placed mankind under two masters, pain and pleasure—and that they alone determine our actions. Accordingly, the purpose of life revolves around the idea that "good" is whatever brings the greatest happiness to the greatest number of people. Bentham called the meaning of life the "greatest happiness principle."

As one can see, these complex "religious" ideas about mankind's ultimate destiny fail to adequately answer the question, *What is the purpose for human existence?* In the end, they merely reflect the vain imaginations of men cut off from the true God, struggling to find an answer to this age-old question.

Chapter One

What the "Intellectual Elite" Believe

The "intellectual elite" of this world—a broad group including secular scholars, atheists, humanists, and philosophers in general—offer little in the way of answering the question, *Why does man exist?* They all share a common starting point: the denial of a Creator and the obstinate adherence to the theory of *evolution*. For them, man is simply the end product of billions of years of an evolutionary process—that all started with a "Big Bang." The universe, the earth, and life itself all accidentally developed from nothing. (See Appendix 1, *Seven Proofs God Exists*.)

Thus, since there is no God, no Creator, there is no *purpose* for human life!

Atheistic evolutionists look to Charles Darwin as the "father" of the theory of evolution, upholding his *Origin of Species* (1860) as their "bible." This theory, however, actually originated with the philosophers of the ancient world. In his article "Evolution: An Ancient Pagan Idea," Paul Griffiths writes: "As I read the works of the Greek philosophers, who lived between about 600-100BC, I was amazed to discover *primitive evolutionary theory*.... The fragments of Anaximander (c. 610–546 BC) taught that 'humans' originally resembled another type of animal, namely fish. There was Democritus (c. 460–370 BC) who taught that primitive people began to speak with 'confused' and 'unintelligible' sounds but 'gradually they articulated words.' Epicurus (341–270 BC) taught that there was no need of a God or gods, for the Universe came about by a chance movement of atoms. After them, the Roman naturalist Pliny the Elder (AD 23–79) said, 'we are so subject to chance that Chance herself takes the place of God; she proves that God is uncertain.'

"The Greeks borrowed some of these ideas from the Babylonians, Egyptians, and Hindus, whose philosophies extended back centuries before. For example, one Hindu belief was that Brahman (the Universe) spontaneously evolved by itself like a seed, which expanded and formed all that exists about 4.3 billion years ago. These Hindus believed in an eternal Universe that had cycles of rebirth, destruction and dormancy, known as 'kalpas', rather like oscillating big bang theories. We also read in the Hindu *Bhagavad Gita* that the god Krishna says, 'I am the source from which all creatures evolve.' " [2]

Like many atheists, *humanists* champion a system of thought that attaches prime importance to *human*, rather than divine, ideals. Humanist beliefs stress the potential value and goodness of human beings, emphasize common human needs, and look to logic in solving human problems. This statement from the *American Humanist Association* summarizes their creed: "Humanism affirms our ability, and responsibility, to lead ethical lives of personal fulfillment that aspire to the greater good of humanity."[3] Concerning the *purpose* of human life, the Association adds: "**People determine human purpose, without supernatural influence; it is the human personality … that is the purpose of a human being's life.**"[4]

Since there is no divine purpose to human life—and nothing beyond death, no afterlife—this *present life* is all-important to the humanist. Again, the beliefs espoused by the elite intellectuals of this world—atheists, evolutionists, humanists—are based on the assumption that there is no God, no divine creation. Thus, for them, there is *no purpose* to human life.

Aldous Huxley (1894-1963) reveals how and why many of these "elite" arrived at this conclusion. In his book *Ends and Means*, he reveals why he and his contemporaries did not believe in God and why they adopted the philosophy of "meaninglessness." He writes: "**I had motives for not wanting the world to have a meaning. Consequently, I assumed that it had none** and I was able without any difficulty to find satisfying reasons for this assumption…. For myself and, no doubt, for most of my contemporaries, **the philosophy of meaninglessness was essentially an instrument of liberation from a certain system of morality**. We objected to the [commonly accepted standard of] morality because it interfered with our sexual freedoms; we objected to the political and economic system because it was unjust…. **There was one admirably simple method of … justifying ourselves in our political and erotic revolt. We could deny that the world had any meaning whatsoever**. Similar tactics had been adopted during the 18th century and for the same reasons…. **The chief reason for being philosophical was that we might be free from prejudices—above all, prejudices of a sexual nature**. It was the manifestly poisonous nature of the fruits that forced me to reconsider the philosophical tree on which they had grown." [5]

Julian Huxley (1887-1975) wrote this concerning his brother: "[Aldous] **saw Humanism** (a word he did use) **as an exact substitute for religion: a worldview based on evolutionary biology**. [Aldous once wrote:] 'This new ideas-system, whose birth we of the mid-twentieth century are witnessing, I shall simply call Humanism, because it can only be based on our understanding of man and his environment. **It must be organized around the facts and ideas of evolution**, taking account of the discovery that man is part of a comprehensive evolutionary process, and cannot avoid playing a decisive role in it.'… [Aldous] added: '[**Humanism**] **will have nothing to do with absolutes, including absolute truth, absolute morality, absolute perfection, and absolute authority**.'…" If, as Huxley once claimed, there is "no other valid kind of knowledge" outside of science, it is a short step to argue, as he did, that we should "invent a new morality based on science." [6]

Presently, the world's leading atheist guru is Richard Dawkins—yet even he asks, in his own contemptuous way, *Why man?* Notice his comment on man's "brief time in the sun." "Isn't it a noble, an enlightened way of spending our brief time in the sun, *to work at understanding the universe and how we have come to wake up in it?* This is how I answer when I am asked—as I am surprisingly often—why I bother to get up in the mornings." [7]

Here are some of Dawkins' cynical thoughts on the "Meaning of Life":

"The universe that we observe has precisely the properties we should expect if there is, at bottom, **no design, no purpose, no evil, no good, nothing but pitiless indifference**." [8]

"There is something infantile in the presumption that somebody else (parents in the case of children, God in the case of adults) **has a responsibility to give your life meaning and point**. Somebody else must be responsible for my well-being, and somebody else must be to blame if I am hurt. **Is it a similar infantilism that really lies behind the 'need' for a God?** The truly adult view is that our life is as meaningful, as full and as wonderful as we choose to make it. And we can make it very wonderful indeed." [9]

"We are made by the laws of physics, working through four billion years of evolution. We have a brief window of life through which to see the universe and understand how we came to be in it. The truth may not always be comforting in the face of suffering, but it has a majesty of its own...."

"It is fashionable to wax apocalyptic about the threat to humanity posed by the AIDS virus, mad cow disease, and many others, but **I think a case can be made that** *faith* **is one of the world's great evils**, comparable to the smallpox virus but harder to eradicate....

"**I think there's something very evil about faith** ... it justifies essentially anything. If you're taught in your holy book or by your priest that blasphemers should die or apostates should die ... that clearly is evil. [But] people don't have to justify it because it's their faith." [10]

Transhumanism: One final subgroup of the secular elite should be mentioned—the proponents of so-called *transhumanism* (sometimes called *posthumanism*). The futuristic idea revolves around "human enhancement." "Basically, it's a sort of re-genesis, [the] altering [of] human bodies—genetically, mechanically, or both—to make them better than they've been for thousands of years, affording them Superman-style abilities in both brains and brawn. Futurists describe it as being 'posthuman,' the next step in what they believe to be the evolutionary process." [11]

This perspective is well explained in Arizona State University's *Templeton Research Lectures*: "Humanity stands now on the precipice of a new phase in human evolution, referred to as 'posthumanism' or 'transhumanism.'...

In the transhuman phase, **humans will become their own makers**, transforming their environment and themselves. Proponents of transhumanism believe that advances in robotics, nanotechnology, artificial intelligence and genomics will liberate humanity from pain and suffering. Presumably, in the transhuman age humanity will conquer the problems of aging, disease, poverty, and hunger, finally actualizing happiness in this life." [12]

It is noted, however, that "those who advocate transhumanism promote a utopian vision rooted in a host of unstated **assumptions about the meaning of being human**." [13] To the contrary, proponents of transhumanism have no clue as to the true purpose of life. Like all atheists, secularists, and humanists, their *creator-less approach* prohibits them from answering the one question that preoccupies man, *What is the purpose of human life?*

Those Who Reject God Cannot Discover, *Why Human Life?*

From the very beginning God has been willing to show mankind His *purpose* for creating the human family. But man has continuously chosen to ignore God's instructions and His revelations. Thus, as we have seen, man has concocted a variety of theories, philosophies and religions in an attempt to answer, *Why is there human life?*

In his epistle to the Romans, Paul describes what happened to ancient religious leaders, intellectuals and philosophers when they rejected the revelation of God. This also is happening to the world's modern societies because like those of ancient times they are rejecting God. Thus Paul's writings are a prophecy against the modern societies of today. He writes: "Indeed, *the* wrath of God is revealed from heaven upon all ungodliness and unrighteousness of **men who suppress the truth in unrighteousness; because that which may be known of God is manifest among them, for God has manifested *it* to them.**

"For the invisible things of Him are **perceived from *the* creation of *the* world, being understood by the things that were made**—both His eternal power and Godhead—so that they are without excuse; **because when they knew God, they glorified *Him* not as God, neither were thankful; but they became vain in their own reasonings, and their foolish hearts were darkened. While professing themselves to be *the* wise ones, they became fools**. And [they] changed the glory of the incorruptible God into *the* likeness of an image of corruptible man, and of birds, and four-footed creatures, and creeping things. **For this cause, God also abandoned them** to uncleanness through the lusts of their hearts, to disgrace their own bodies between themselves, **who exchanged the truth of God for the lie; and they worshiped and served the created thing** more than the One Who is

Creator, Who is blessed into the ages. Amen" (Rom 1:18-25).

Nearly 1,200 years earlier, King David, a righteous man after God's own heart, wrote that those who reject and deny God are indeed fools: "**The fool has said in his heart, 'There is no God.'** They are corrupt, and have worked out abominable wickedness; there is no one who does good. God looked down from heaven upon the children of men to see if there were any who understand, who are seeking after God. **Every one has turned away; they have altogether become corrupt; no one is doing good, no, not even one. Will the workers of iniquity never learn?**" (Psa. 53:1-4).

In exercising "free moral agency," mankind as a whole has chosen to reject God and has refused to listen to His word. As a result, their hearts and minds are blinded. As Jesus said, "[God] has blinded their eyes and hardened their hearts so that they would not see with *their* eyes and understand with *their* hearts…" (John 12:40).

In this state of spiritual blindness, men convince themselves that they are wise, intelligent and competent. But Proverbs tell us: "There is **a way that seems right to a man**, but the end thereof is the way of death…. All the ways of a man are clean in his own eyes…. The way of a fool *is* right in his own eyes" (Prov. 16:25; 16:2; 12:15).

Apart from God and His word, it is impossible for men to know even *how to live* as our Maker intended. As Jeremiah acknowledged, "O LORD, **I know that the way of man is not in himself;** *it is* **not in man who walks to direct his steps**" (Jer. 10:23). Likewise, apart from God and His revealed word, it is impossible for man to answer the most fundamental questions of life: *What is the purpose of human existence? What is man's place in the universe? Is there life beyond the grave? What is our ultimate destiny? Why was I born?*

Because mankind has chosen to ignore God and devise their own societies and religions, God has, in turn, chosen to *hide* His purpose for human life. Jesus said: "I praise You, O Father, Lord of heaven and earth, that You did hide these [secret] things from *the* wise and intelligent…" (Luke 10:21).

But *where* has God hidden this secret knowledge? It is "hidden" in the Scriptures, identified as the "mystery of God"—the "mystery that has been hidden from ages and generations" (Col. 2:2; 1:26).

Indeed, the "glory of God *is* to conceal a thing, but the honor of kings *is* to search out a matter" (Prov. 25:2). As we will see in the next chapter, God has hidden this knowledge "in plain sight"—yet only He can reveal it, only He can answer the pivotal question, *Why were you born?*

Chapter 1 Notes:

1. Sources: Adherents.com, Religionfacts.com, Wikipedia.com, Beliefnet.com, ReligiousTolerance.org, Omsakthi.org, and jewfaq.org

2. www.creation.com/evolution-ancient-pagan-idea

3. *Humanist Manifesto III: Humanism and Its Aspirations*, American Humanist Association

4. *Humanist Manifesto I;* emphasis added

5. Aldous Huxley, *Ends and Means*, 1937. From the section *Reasons and Denial of a Special Creation of Everything for Explanation of Creation Without a Divine Creator*, pp. 312, 315, 316, 318; emphasis added.

6. www.aeon.co/magazine/philosophy/michael-ruse-humanism-religion; emphasis added

7. Richard Dawkins, *Unweaving the Rainbow—Science, Delusion and the Appetite for Wonder*; emphasis added

8. Dawkins, *River Out of Eden—A Darwinian View of Life*; emphasis added

9. Dawkins, *The God Delusion*; emphasis added

10. Dawkins, "Sex, Death, and the Meaning of Life" (documentary); emphasis added

11. www.wnd.com/index.php?fa=PAGE.view&pageId=346993; emphasis added

12. Arizona State University *Templeton Research Lectures,* "Facing the Challenges of Transhumanism"; www.transhumanism.asu.edu; emphasis added

13. *ibid*

CHAPTER TWO

Where Do We Begin?

As we have seen, the "intellectual elite"—humanists, atheists, evolutionists and philosophers—have their sundry theories on the origins and purpose of human life. But in their vanity, they have *wholly dismissed*—even *rejected*— the ultimate source of vital knowledge, the Holy Scriptures. Having never honestly proven the Bible, they reject it—convinced it is filled with myths, fairytales and fables from the minds of men. In arrogance they rebuff those who believe the Bible is actually the revealed Word of God—written by men under the *inspiration* of God.

Of all the writings and books men have composed throughout history, none can be compared to the Scriptures. [1] Only the Bible contains the *revealed truth* of God—and God cannot lie (Titus 1:2; Heb. 6:18). Jesus said of the Word of God, "Your word is the truth" (John 17:17).

But what is the Bible really? It is God's *personal message* to you, to me—to all of mankind! It alone reveals the *purpose* for human life!

God literally wrote the Ten Commandments on stone tablets with His finger (Ex. 31:18). But for the remainder of the Scriptures, God carefully chose men who loved and feared Him and *inspired them* through His Spirit to compose the Word of God. [2] The apostle Peter writes that the Scriptures are not humanly devised myths based on the imaginations of men: "For we did not follow cleverly concocted myths *as our authority*, when we made known to you the power and coming of our Lord Jesus Christ, but we were eyewitnesses of His magnificent glory.... We also possess the confirmed prophetic Word [the teachings of Christ] to which you do well to pay attention, as to a light shining in a dark place ... knowing this first, that **no prophecy of Scripture originated as anyone's own *private* interpretation; because prophecy was not brought at any time by human will, but the holy men of God spoke as they were moved by *the* Holy Spirit**" (II Pet. 1:16, 19-21).

The apostle Paul substantiates the divine inspiration of the Scriptures, when he wrote to Timothy: "And that from a child you have known the Holy Writings [Old Testament], which are able to make you wise unto salvation through faith, which *is* in Christ Jesus. **All Scripture** [Old and New Testaments] *is* **God-breathed** and *is* profitable for doctrine, for conviction, for correction, for instruction in righteousness" (II Tim 3:15-16).

In the Greek, "God-breathed" literally means "God-spirited." Thus, *each* and *every passage* is "God-spirited." This completely separates the Bible from all other writings! God inspired—*spirited* with His Holy Spirit—the words of the Scriptures. When faithfully translated into other languages, the spiritual meaning and power of the inspired original is carried over into the translated text. This is why Jesus said, "It is the Spirit that gives life…. **The words that I speak to you,** *they* **are spirit and** *they* **are life**" (John 6:63)—and "It is written, 'Man shall not live by bread alone, but by every word that proceeds out of *the* mouth of God' " (Matt. 4:4). [3]

Only the Scriptures reveal the awesome divine purpose for mankind's existence. But, in His infinite wisdom, God has *hidden* this truth "in plain sight" right on the pages of the Bible. *Why?* Because most people do not want to follow God's way of life; instead, they want to follow the ways of this evil world, with all of its materialistic pleasures. God has determined that He will reveal the incredible purpose for human life *only* to those who fear Him—who obey Him. The Scriptures themselves reveal the keys that unlock God's hidden purpose and plan for mankind. Thus, if we are to understand the *purpose for human life*, we must revere and submit to the Word of God—His personal revelation to mankind.

Have You Too Been Deceived?

Modern Christians profess a belief in God, and even acknowledge that He created all things. Research, however, shows that most so-called Christians largely pay lip-service to God; from a practical standpoint, they are *indistinguishable* from non-Christians. [4]

Most Christians entertain vague ideas of one day "going to heaven." They are blinded, *deceived*, as to the true destiny of mankind. Why? Because they have no real regard for the teachings of the Bible (Isa. 5:24). Notice what Isaiah writes: "Be stunned and amazed! **Blind your eyes and be blind!** They [today's so-called Christians] are drunk, but not with wine; they stagger, but not *with* strong drink, **for the LORD has poured out upon you the spirit of deep sleep, and has closed your eyes; He has covered the prophets** [your teachers and pastors] **and your rulers,** *and* **the seers**. And the vision of all has become to you like the words of a book that is sealed, which they give to one who is learned [the so-called Bible scholar] saying, 'Please read this,' and he says, 'I cannot, for it is sealed.' And the book is delivered to him who is not learned [the ordinary man or woman], saying, 'Please read this,' and he says, 'I am not learned.'

"And the LORD said, '**Because this people** [today's "Christian" church-goer] **draws near** *Me* **with their mouth, and with their lips honor Me** [they *say* all the right-sounding things], **but their worship of Me is made up of the traditions of men learned by rote, and their fear toward Me is *taught* by the commandments of men**; therefore, behold, I will proceed to do again a marvelous work among this people, *even* a marvelous work and a wonder, for the wisdom of their wise ones shall perish, and the wisdom of their intelligent ones shall vanish' " (Isa. 29:9-14).

What a resounding indictment on modern Christianity—with its manmade traditions and its obsession with worldliness. Referencing Isaiah, Jesus said, "Well did Isaiah prophesy concerning you hypocrites, as it is written, 'This people honors Me with their lips, but **their hearts are far away from Me. But in vain do they worship Me, teaching *for* doctrine the commandments of men.' For leaving the commandment of God, you hold fast the tradition of men**" (Mark 7:5-8).

Spiritual blindness is the result of a false "conversion"—by a false "Christianity" based on human tradition and the near total disregard for the laws and commandments of God. When was the last time you heard a Sunday morning sermon on *overcoming sin*, on *obeying God* in every area of our lives, on being *totally different* from the world? You *won't* hear such a message in mainstream Christianity—because it doesn't fill pews and it won't pay the pastor's salary! What you will hear is a feel-good "Gospel" proclaiming that "Jesus has already done it all for you."

Your Bible teaches that true understanding comes only to those who obey God. The way to overcome spiritual blindness is to return to God by seeking Him in *repentance*. And we have to come to God on *His* terms! "Seek the LORD while He may be found; call upon Him while He is near. Let the wicked forsake his way, and the unrighteous man his thoughts; and let him return to the LORD, and He will have mercy upon him; and to our God, for He will abundantly pardon. 'For My thoughts *are* not your thoughts, nor your ways My ways,' says the LORD. 'For *as* the heavens are higher than the earth, so are My ways higher than your ways, and My thoughts than your thoughts' " (Isa. 55:6-9).

How do we return to God? *First*, we must repent of our sins, which are the transgressions of God's Law (I John 3:4). *Second*, we begin to keep the commandments of God (I John 2:3-6). *Third*, we begin to love God, as the apostle John writes: "For this is the love of God: that we keep His commandments; and His commandments are not burdensome" (I John 5:3). Jesus also said, "If you love Me, keep the commandments—namely, My commandments" (John 14:15).

When we love and fear God, He will grant us spiritual understanding: "The fear of the LORD is the beginning of wisdom; **a good understanding have all those who do** [keep or practice] **His commandments**" (Psa.

111:10). Again, God tells us that by loving and fearing Him, we will be blessed with wisdom and understanding: "The fear of the LORD *is* the beginning of wisdom; and the knowledge of the holy *is* understanding" (Prov. 9:10).

Those who truly *fear God*—who draw close to Him in loving obedience—will be given the knowledge of his plan for mankind. Notice: "**The secret of the LORD is with those who fear Him, and He will show them His covenant** [which reveals God's plan and purpose for mankind]" (Psa. 25:14). And again, "For the crooked man *is* an abomination to the LORD, but **His secret *is* with the righteous**" (Prov.3:32).

You *Can* Understand!

After Jesus was resurrected from the dead, He opened the minds of His disciples to understand the Scriptures: "And He said to them, 'These *are* the words that I spoke to you when I was yet with you, that all *the* things which were written concerning Me in the Law of Moses and *in the* Prophets and *in the* Psalms must be fulfilled.' **Then He opened their minds to understand the Scriptures**..." (Luke 24:44-45). Again as David wrote, "**Open my eyes, so that I may behold wondrous things out of Your law**" (Psa. 119:18).

God is *most willing* to open your eyes to the truth of His word—the truth of *why* He created humankind! But you have your part, and obedience is the key. Righteousness *is* the keeping of God's commandments (Psa. 119:172), starting with the Ten Commandments, which are easy to understand (Ex. 20:1-17; Deut. 5:6-21). God's laws and commandments are living principles that you will come to fully understand *only by keeping them*. You will learn that God's commandments are based on *love*—toward God *and* toward neighbor (Matt. 22:36-40).

With this as your foundation, God will begin to lift the spiritual blindness that plagues so many professing Christians today. He will *open your mind* to comprehend the Word of God.

While many passages in the Bible are easy to understand, others are admittedly difficult. But God has given us definite *keys* to discover and understand the secrets hidden in His word. As you progress through this book, keep these vital principles in mind:

First, realize that key passages concerning the hidden things of God are *not all written in one place*. Rather, they are scattered "here a little, there a little" throughout the entire Bible. It is our job to *search them out* as we "examine the Scriptures" (Acts 17:11). Isaiah writes: "**Whom shall He [God] teach knowledge? And whom shall He make to understand doctrine?** *Those* who are weaned from the milk and drawn from the breasts..." (Isa. 28:9). This means God will impart understanding only to those *grounded in the fundamental things* of the Word of God—no longer needing the *milk* of the word only (I Pet. 2:2-4). Isaiah continues, showing how God has inspired the hidden things of His word to be written: "For precept *must be* upon precept, precept upon precept; line upon line, line upon line; **here a little, there a little**" (verse 10). This is how God has *hidden* His secrets—even the deep things of God—in various places throughout the Bible. Indeed, we must "search the Scriptures" to find these truths.

Searching the Bible—*bringing relevant passages together*—is what Paul called "rightly dividing" the Word of God. He admonished Timothy: "Give careful consideration to the things *that* I am telling you, and **may the Lord give you understanding in all things**…. **Diligently** *study* **to show yourself approved unto God**, a workman who does not *need to be* ashamed, **rightly dividing the Word of the truth**" (II Tim. 2:7, 15). As we gather the various relevant passages together, we will begin to comprehend the full meaning of what God has purposed for the human family.

Paul brings out another vital factor in our righteous use of the Scriptures. He explains that the *Word* of God and the *Spirit* of God work hand-in-hand—because the words of God are "spirit and life." This means that without the guidance and inspiration of the Holy Spirit, you cannot understand the deeper things of God. "Now we speak wisdom among the *spiritually* mature [those who submit to God in loving obedience]; however, *it is* not *the* [intellectual] wisdom of this [secular] world, nor of the rulers [or scholars] of this world, who are coming to nothing. Rather, **we speak** *the* **wisdom of God in a mystery,** *even* **the hidden** *wisdom* **that God foreordained before the ages unto our glory**, which not one of the rulers [or intellectuals] of this world has known (for if they had known, they would not have crucified the Lord of glory);

"But according as it is written, '*The* eye has not seen, nor *the* ear heard, neither have entered into *the* heart of man, *the* things which God has prepared for those who love Him.' But **God has revealed** *them* **to us by His Spirit, for the Spirit searches all things—even the deep things of God.** For who among men understands the things of man except *by* the spirit of man which *is* in him? In the same way also, **the things of God no one understands except** *by* **the Spirit of God.** Now we have not received the spirit of the world [with its human wisdom], but the Spirit that *is* of God, **so that we might know the things graciously given to us by God**; which things we also speak, not in words taught by human wisdom, but in *words* taught by *the* Holy Spirit *in order to* communicate spiritual things by spiritual *means*. **But** *the* **natural man** [with an unconverted mind] **does not receive the things of the Spirit of God; for they are foolishness to him, and he**

cannot understand *them* **because they are spiritually discerned**" (I Cor. 2:6-14).

In the following chapters we will apply these principles of "searching out" and "rightly dividing" the Word of God. As we do so, we will begin to understand God's incredible purpose for creating mankind!

Chapter 2 Notes:

1. The Bible remains the all-time number-one-selling book—and there are more Bibles available today than ever. Since the first printing of the Bible in 1450 AD, nearly *seven billion* Bibles have been published, with the majority of them still available for use.

The complete Bible has been translated into over 450 languages; the New Testament alone has been translated into nearly 1,500 languages and the Gospel of Mark into over 2,000 languages. Today, the Bible, in whole or in part, is available on the Internet from hundreds of Web sites. This makes it downloadable to any digital device anywhere in the world—24/7. With digital devices already numbering in the billions, access to the Bible is virtually unlimited. This universal availability of the Scriptures is no doubt a key element in reaching the entire world with the Gospel (Mark 13:10; Matt. 24:14; Acts 1:8).

2. Over a period of some 4,000 years, God used only 40 men to write the entire Bible. For the Old Testament, originally written in Hebrew, God used Moses, the prophets, and some of the ancient kings of Israel. For the New Testament, originally written in *koine* Greek, He used only *eight* men—all chosen and taught by Christ.

3. The Word of God is *active* and *living* at all times, because it has the power of God's Spirit behind it. Paul notes: "**For the Word of God** *is* **living and powerful**, and sharper than any two-edged sword, piercing even to the dividing asunder of both soul and spirit, *and* of both *the* joints and *the* marrow, and *is* able to discern *the* thoughts and intents of *the* heart " (Heb. 4:12). No other book in the world can do this!

God's word works hand-in-hand with His *laws*—which are as inexorable as the "law of gravity." Thus, when we love and obey God, as written in His word, blessings automatically result. But when we reject God and His word—and break His laws, which is sin—the automatic results are judgments and curses.

4. Please refer to our booklet *Why Is Christianity Failing in America?*

CHAPTER THREE

Man and Woman Created
in God's *Image* and *Likeness*

Genesis chapter one contains the account of God's preparation of the earth for mankind. On the first five days, God set in motion day and night, created the firmament above the earth, established the waters below, and made the dry land and all vegetation. He then "set" the sun and moon in their proper positions for His appointed times. Next He created all birds and sea life, beasts, crawling things, and insects. By the power of His *word*, He brought all of them into existence: *"God said"*—and they came into being. Of the plants, fish, birds, and animals of every kind, God created them with the ability to reproduce and perpetuate their *own kind*—and He commanded them to "be fruitful and multiply."

On the other hand, when God created man and woman, He did not "command" them into existence. Rather, He personally *formed* them with His own hands in *His own image*—giving them abilities and qualities after His likeness.

Beginning in verse 26, God gives us a summary of His creation of man and woman: "And God said, '**Let Us make man in Our image, after Our likeness**....' " As we will learn later from other passages in the Bible, this special creation of man and woman formed the foundation for the fulfillment of God's plan and purpose for the entire human family.

The fact that God created mankind in His *own image* is most profound! Indeed, for emphasis God repeats Himself in the next verse: "**And God created man in His *own* image, in the image of God He created him. He created them male and female**..." (verse 27). God then reveals that He had put the entire world   including *everything* He had created—into their hands and under their rulership. He said: "And let them have dominion over the fish of the sea and over the fowl of heaven and over the livestock and over all the earth and over every creeping thing that crawls upon the earth ... And God blessed them. And God said to them, 'Be fruitful and multiply, and replenish the earth, and subdue it; and have dominion over the fish of the sea and over the fowl of heaven and over every living thing that moves upon the earth' " (verses 26, 28).

Then God surveyed all that He had created: "And God saw everything that He had made, and indeed, *it was exceedingly* good. And the evening

16

and the morning were the sixth day…. Thus, the heavens and the earth were finished, and all the host of them" (Gen. 1:31-2:1). [1]

In chapter two, God provides us with the details of how He created the first man and woman—Adam and Eve. "Then the LORD God formed man *of the* dust of the ground, and breathed into his nostrils the breath of life; and man became a living being" (verse 7).

God also created a beautiful Paradise for them to live in, the Garden of Eden. After God created Adam, He placed him in the garden: "And the LORD God planted a garden eastward in Eden; and there He put the man whom He had formed [to dress and keep it; to keep also means to guard (verse15)]. And out of the ground the LORD God caused to grow every tree that is pleasant to the sight and good for food. **The tree of life also was in the middle of the garden, and the tree of** *the* **knowledge of good and evil**" (verses 8-9).

"And the LORD God commanded the man, saying, 'You may freely eat of every tree in the garden, but you shall not eat of the tree of *the* knowledge of good and evil, for in the day that you eat of it, in dying you shall surely die.' And the LORD God said, '*It is* not good that the man should be alone. I will make a helper [a counterpart, or sustainer, beside him and] compatible for him.' And out of the ground the LORD God *had* formed [by His commands] every animal of the field and every fowl of the air—and brought *them* to Adam to see what he would call them. And whatever Adam called *each* living creature, that *became* its name. And Adam gave names to all the livestock, and to the birds of the air, and to every animal of the field, but there was not found a helper compatible for Adam" (verses 16-20).

From this account we can conclude that God created Adam with a full, working language so that he could think and communicate with His Creator. In naming all the creatures God had created, Adam would quickly realize that they were all male and female and that they could produce offspring according to their own kind. He would also realize that there was no compatible female for himself.

God then made Eve as the perfect counterpart for Adam. However, God did not create the woman from the dust of the earth. Rather, He made Eve from one of Adam's ribs: "And the LORD God caused a deep sleep to fall over Adam, and he slept. And He took one of his ribs, and *afterward* closed up the flesh underneath. Then the LORD God made [built] the rib (which He had taken out of the man) into a woman, and He brought her to the man.

"And Adam said, 'This *is* now bone of my bones and flesh of my flesh. *She* shall be called Woman because *she* was taken out of Man.' For this reason shall a man leave his father and his mother, and shall cleave to his wife—and they shall become one flesh. And they were both naked, the man and his wife, and they were not ashamed" (verses 21-25). Adam and Eve walked and talked with God. Since their minds were innocent, they were not ashamed of being naked in God's presence.[2]

God created man in His *own* image and after His *own* likeness. Of all that God created, man and woman alone were made with His own hands. Indeed, from the beginning, God reveals the magnitude of His love for man and woman—the pinnacle of His earthly creation! Now, as husband and wife, Adam and Eve had the ability, through a loving sexual union, to bring forth children after *their* kind, in *their* image—which is the image and likeness of God. He particularly made the man to be the *progenitor*, to beget new human life. He especially made the woman to be able to *conceive*, develop and sustain new offspring within her own body. Moreover, after giving birth, she is to be the nurturer and sustainer of each new child. Thus, men and women are truly *partners with God* in creating human life.

In fact, from the beginning, by His creation of man and woman, God *established the family unit*—father, mother and children. They and their offspring would multiply and replenish the earth as God commanded. Thus, knowingly or unknowingly, all mankind is actively participating in God's plan by bringing forth billions of human beings—all in God's image and likeness—through the power of procreation.

A Choice Between Two Ways of Life

Being made in the image and likeness of God does not mean that Adam and Eve were created with robotic instincts. In addition to possessing godlike characteristics, God created man and woman as free moral agents with the power of independent choice. Of course, God *instructed* Adam and set before him clear choices. And God also warned of the *consequences* for making the wrong choice: "And the LORD God commanded the man, saying, **'You may freely eat of every tree in the garden, but you shall not eat of the tree of *the* knowledge of good and evil, for in the day that you eat of it in dying you shall surely die'** " (Gen. 2:16-17). The phrase "in dying you shall surely die" did not mean immediate death if they ate of the forbidden tree; rather, they would *definitely* die at some point in the future.

As we will see, *every* human being from that time forward has been given this capacity to choose. The choice each one of us must make is quite straightforward: *love* and *obey God*—or not. As Creator and Lawgiver, God has decreed that the *penalty* for disobedience to His instructions is death. But through *faith*—if one comes to love and obey God—He will grant the gift of eternal life. This was the choice God set before Adam and Eve, as depicted by the two trees in the Garden of Eden—the "tree of life" and the "tree of the knowledge of good and evil."

Adam and Eve were created in a state of innocence. They were sinless and blameless before God. Prior to eating of the forbidden fruit, they were not subject to the penalty of death. But neither did they have eternal life, because they were made of the dust of the earth. However, they could have inherited eternal life by choosing to love and obey God; *then* they could have eaten of the "tree of life." Instead, they chose to take matters into their own hands and to disobey God by eating of the "tree of the knowledge of good and evil." As we will see, their choice has affected all of mankind. If Adam and Eve had chosen to love and obey God and had eaten of the "tree of life," what a different world it would have been! [3]

Adam and Eve Choose the Way of Sin

Genesis records that Adam and Eve received God's instructions before the serpent, Satan the devil, was allowed to test them so that God could *see* which way they would choose—the way that leads to eternal life, or the way that leads to sin and death (Gen. 2:16-17). Since they had been in personal contact with God, their knowledge of His instructions was direct and firsthand. Thus, they could never have said, "Lord, I didn't know."

Notice the account in Genesis three: "Now the serpent was more cunning than any creature of the field which the LORD God had made. And he said to the woman, '*Is it* true that God has said, "You shall not eat of any tree of the garden?" ' And the woman said to the serpent, 'We may freely eat the fruit of the trees of the garden, but of the fruit of the tree which *is* in the middle of the garden, God has *indeed* said, "You shall not eat of it, neither shall you touch it, lest you die" ' " (verses 1-3).

As the biblical record reveals, Eve had full knowledge of God's instructions and commands concerning the "tree of the knowledge of good and evil." But in spite of this, Eve listened to the serpent: "And the serpent said to the woman, 'In dying, you shall not surely die! For God knows that in the day you eat of it, then your eyes shall be opened, and you shall be like God, deciding good and evil' " (verses 4-5).

Instead of rejecting the arguments of the serpent by believing and obeying God, Eve took some of the fruit and ate it, and then gave some to Adam: "And when the woman saw that the tree *was* good for food, and that it was pleasing to the eyes, and a tree to be desired to make *one* wise, she took of its fruit and ate. She also gave to her husband with her, and he ate" (verse 6).

The Consequences of Adam and Eve's Sin

As a result of their disobedience to God, Adam and Eve were no longer innocent, but became sinful: "**And the eyes both of them were opened** [to decide for themselves what is good and evil], **and they knew that they *were* naked**; and they sewed fig leaves together and made coverings for themselves" (Gen. 3:7).

When Adam and Eve ate of the fruit of the "tree of the knowledge of good and evil," sin entered into the human realm. With this first act of disobedience, sin became part of the human mind and being. Adam and Eve now had a sinful nature—a mixture of good and evil.

Before they sinned, Adam and Eve were not afraid of God. They walked and talked with God and were not ashamed of being naked in His presence. But after they sinned, their thoughts became a mixture of good and evil, and they became ashamed that they were naked; they became afraid of God. "And they heard the sound of the LORD God walking in the garden in the cool of the day. Then Adam and his wife hid themselves from the presence of the LORD God among the trees of the garden. And the LORD God called to Adam, and said to him, 'Where *are* you?' And he said, I heard you *walking* in the garden, and I was afraid, because I *am* naked, and *so* I hid myself.' And He said, 'Who told you that you *were* naked? Have you eaten of the tree which I commanded you that you should not eat?' " (verses 8-11).

Rather than admitting his sin, Adam blamed his wife, Eve. By doing so he was, in effect, blaming God, because He created Eve and gave her to Adam: "And the man said, 'The woman whom You gave *to be* with me, she gave me of the tree, and I ate' " (verse 12). Likewise, Eve did not admit her sin of picking and eating the forbidden fruit, and giving it to Adam to eat. She blamed the serpent: "And the LORD God said to the woman, 'What *is* this you have done?' And the woman said, 'The serpent deceived me, and I ate' " (verse 13).

God then rendered His judgment against them, starting with the serpent: "And the LORD God said to the serpent, 'Because you have done this you *are* cursed above all livestock, and above every animal of the field. You shall go upon your belly, and you shall eat dust all the days of your life' " (verse 14).

In pronouncing His judgment against the serpent, God also introduced the promise of the Messiah, who would be born of a woman. Thus, God made a way for the atoning of the sins of all mankind, beginning with Adam and Eve. [4] Ultimately, the Messiah would also destroy all the works of the serpent, passing eternal judgment on Satan the devil (Heb. 2:14; Matt. 25:41; Rev. 20:10).

God's judgment here in Genesis against the serpent hints at the conflict that would eventually develop between Satan and God's Church. "And I will put enmity between you [the serpent] and the woman [the coming Church of God], and between your seed [the demons and those who would serve Satan] and her Seed [the coming Messiah]; He [Christ] will bruise your head, and you [Satan] shall bruise His heel [through the crucifixion]" (verse 15). (See Appendix 2, *Did God Create Satan the Devil?*)

The sin of Adam and Eve had profound consequences, for them and for all humanity. God's judgment was upon them, upon the earth, and upon all future human beings. Notice God's judgment upon Adam and Eve: "To the woman He said, 'I will greatly multiply your sorrow and your conception—in sorrow you shall bring forth children; your desire shall be toward your husband, and he shall rule over you.' And to Adam He said, 'Because you have hearkened to the voice of your wife, and have eaten of the tree—of which I commanded you, saying, "You shall not eat *of* it!"—the ground *is* cursed for your sake. In sorrow shall you eat of it all the days of your life. It shall also bring forth thorns and thistles to you; and *thus* you shall eat the herb of the field; in the sweat of your face you shall eat bread, until you return to the ground, for out of it you were taken; **for dust you** *are*, **and to dust you shall return'** " (verses 16-19).

Indeed, God's judgment included the sentence of *death*. However, the sentence was not imposed immediately, and Adam and Eve were allowed to live hundreds of years. Genesis does not mention how long Eve lived, but records the length of Adam's life: "And all the days that Adam lived were nine hundred and thirty years. And he died" (Gen. 5:5).

As a result of their sin, Adam and Eve were *exiled* from the Garden of Eden, cutting them off from access to the "tree of life" and from receiving the Holy Spirit of God, which imparts the power to live forever (Gen. 3:24). Furthermore, their sinful nature was passed on *genetically* to all their descendants, who were also cut off from access to the Holy Spirit. Without the Holy Spirit of God, mankind has very little power to resist the temptations of the flesh and the influence of Satan the devil, who now became the "god of this world" (II Cor. 4:4).

From that time on, all of mankind would be subject to the inner "law of sin and death" (Rom. 8:2). It is a fact that **no human being can escape the death that Adam brought upon all mankind**: "Therefore, as by one man sin entered into the world, and by means of sin *came* death; and in this way, **death passed into all mankind**; *and it is* for this reason that all have sinned" (Rom. 5:12). "For in Adam we all die" (I Cor. 15:22). Again, it is written that "it is appointed to men once to die" (Heb. 9:27).

Chapter Three

Adam and Eve Retained Their God-like Attributes

As a consequence of their sin, Adam and Eve could no longer dwell with God in the Garden of Eden. They could, however, *meet with God* at the east entrance of the garden, probably at certain set times. While the "law of sin and death" became a part of their nature, God did not take away their god-like attributes. Thus, God undoubtedly continued to teach them.

Most importantly, man was still created in God's *image* and after His *likeness*. Indeed, only human beings have been given attributes of God—including the ability to think and reason, to speak and write, to plan, create and build, to teach and learn, to judge and rule. God gave human beings the capacity to love, to hate, to laugh, to cry, to forgive, to *repent*, and to experience every type of emotion. All these qualities are godlike characteristics which mankind alone is privileged to possess, though made of flesh and quite inferior to God.

In one of his Psalms praising God, King David begins to reveal *why* God created man in His image and likeness. David was inspired to write, "O LORD our Lord, how excellent is Your name in all the earth! You have set Your glory above the heavens.... When I consider Your heavens, the work of Your fingers, the moon and the stars which You have ordained, [I am compelled to ask,] **what is man that You are mindful of him.... You have made him a little lower than God** [Hebrew *Elohim*]..." (Psa. 8:1-5).

What a profound statement! Mankind was made a little lower than *Elohim*, or God! Unable to believe this astonishing statement, many translators of the Bible (including those of the *King James Version*) incorrectly render this verse as "a little lower than the angels." However, the Hebrew *Elohim* refers to deities—not to angels (the Hebrew word for angels is *malak*). *Elohim* is used countless times in the Hebrew text in reference to the true God, as well to false gods. In every other occurrence in the *King James Version*, *Elohim* is correctly translated "God" or "gods." In Psalm 8:5, this Hebrew word is clearly referring to the true God and should be translated accordingly. Green's translation attempts to convey the meaning of the text this way: "For You have made him lack a little from God...."[5]

How is it that human beings are "a little lower than God"? What did God create in man that sets us apart from other forms of life? How is it possible that man alone possesses godlike attributes?

The Spirit of Man

God is composed of *spirit* (John 4:24). And from God comes the Holy Spirit, which is the *power* of God through which He does all things. The

Bible also reveals that God has given to each person a separate, invisible *spirit essence* or *substance* called the "spirit of man" (or the "spirit in man"). God gives this special spirit at conception. Its purpose is to enable humans to have *thought* and *consciousness*. "But *there is* a **spirit in man** and the inspiration of the Almighty gives them understanding" (Job 32:8). The apostle Paul notes its unique function: "For who among men understands the things of men except *by* **the spirit of man which** *is* **in him**?" (I Cor. 2:11.)

The *spirit of man*, though unseen, is *united* with the human brain. It is not a separate spirit *being*, such as an angel or demon. Rather, it is a spirit *essence* or *substance* that God places *in* each person. It imparts the power of life, thought, intellect, and other godlike characteristics. This human spirit makes man and woman different from any other creature God has created. The prophet Isaiah writes that God has "created the heavens and stretched them out, spreading forth the earth and its offspring." Continuing, God "gives breath [life] to the people upon [the earth] and [gives] **spirit** [Hebrew, *ruach*] to those who walk in it" (Isa. 42:5). God places this spirit essence within each human being: "Thus says the LORD, Who stretches forth the heavens, and lays the foundation of the earth, and forms **the spirit** [*ruach*] **of man within him**" (Zech. 12:1).

This *spirit of man* enables human beings to possess numerous godlike attributes. Indeed, it is this *unique spiritual dimension* that makes us "a little lower than God."

However, the "spirit of man" is *different* from what the Bible calls the "soul."

The word "soul" is translated from the Hebrew *nephesh*, meaning *physical life*, whether human or animal. In many Bible passages, *nephesh* is translated "creature" or "life" (Gen. 1:20-21, 24, 30; 2:19; 9:4-5, 10, 12, 15-16; etc.). When translated "soul," it refers to the *physical life* and strength of a human being (Gen. 2:7; Ex. 1:5; Lev. 23:27; Deut. 4:29; Joshua 11:11; etc.).

Rather than being *separate from* the physical body, the soul is inextricably fused *with* the body. When God created Adam from the dust of the ground, Adam did not *receive* a soul, he "*became* a living soul" (*nephesh*). The "soul" is what a person *is* physically—not something he "has." The "soul" empowers the physical functions of the body—the blood, lymph, and nerve systems of each person. Indeed, the "soul" can *die* (Ezek. 13:18-19; 18:4, 20). Nearly all *living* animals are referred to as "souls" because they have physical life. The Bible tells us that their "souls" die as well (Rev. 16:3).

Paul writes that there are three aspects to human life: "Now may the God of peace Himself sanctify you wholly; and may your entire [human] **spirit** and **soul** [life] and [physical] **body** be preserved blameless unto the coming of our Lord Jesus Christ" (I Thess. 5:23)

Unlike the soul, which *ends* with the death of the body, the "spirit in man" *returns to God* when a person dies (Eccl. 12:7). Importantly, the "spirit of man" contains a *complete record* of the thoughts, memories, and character of the person to whom it belonged. Upon a person's death, God *preserves* this human spirit—to use it again at the resurrection in order to fully restore the person with a new body and mind.

Referring to those who will be in the first resurrection to eternal life, Paul speaks of the "**spirits of the just who have been perfected**" (Heb. 12:23). Indeed, it is the *completed* "spirit of man" that God will use to resurrect those who will be in the first resurrection. (See Appendix 3, *What Happens After Death?*)

In Chapter Four we will see that God's creation of human beings is *continuing* through human procreation. Because this is a major part of God's plan for mankind, He is more directly involved in this process than people have ever imagined.

Chapter 3 Notes:

1. While the work of preparing the heavens and the earth for mankind was completed in six days, God had yet another special aspect to add to His creation—the seventh-day Sabbath. Since God had already created day and night, He created the Sabbath by *resting* on that day—by putting His presence into the day, blessing it and setting it apart as *holy time*, designating it as a day of *fellowship* between the Creator God and mankind. Thus, the Sabbath day is a perpetual reminder that God alone is Creator: "And by *the beginning of* the seventh day God finished His work which He had made. And He rested on the seventh day from all His work which He had made. **And God blessed the seventh day and sanctified it** because on it He rested from all His work which God had created and made" (Gen 2:1-3).

Thus, the seventh-day Sabbath became a day to rest and worship God. **It is holy time, because God blessed and sanctified it for all time**. God has never changed the Sabbath day! At creation, God established the seven-day week; it remains intact, and He has never changed the day of worship to the first day of the week. God created time, and He calculates time—days, weeks, months and years—according to *His* sacred Calculated Hebrew Calendar.

For a complete study of the Sabbath/Sunday controversy, request the booklets *Which Day is the True Lord's Day—Sabbath or Sunday?* and *A Sabbath-Sunday Controversy You Have Never Read.* These are available at no cost.

2. In order for Adam and Eve to be in the presence of God—walking and talking with Him—it is obvious that He did not appear in His glorified form, as no man can see His face and live. When talking with Moses, God told him: "You cannot see My face, for no man can see Me [in My glory] and live" (Ex. 33:20). Therefore, though God is composed of Spirit and possesses an unfathomable glory, He must have appeared to Adam and Eve in a human-like form.

3. To answer the question *What Would the World Be Like if Adam and Eve had Not Sinned?,* you may request our CD message with that title.

4. Jesus the Messiah would also be called "the Lamb of God, slain from the foundation of the world" (Rev. 13:8). However, it would be over 4,000 years from the time of Adam to the Messiah's coming. Beginning with Adam and Eve, God provided atonement for sin through the use of sacrificial animals. From the account in Genesis three, God apparently made atonement for them by sacrificing goats at the east entrance of the Garden of Eden. He then made coverings for them from the skins.

After God expelled Adam and Eve from the Garden of Eden, He placed cherubim at the east entrance to prevent man from reentering (verses 21, 23-24). While men could no longer dwell with God in the garden, they could come before Him at the east gate, where they could communicate with Him and receive instruction. There must have been an altar at this gate, because Abel offered firstlings of his flock to God. We also find that God talked with Cain about his improper offering. This shows that God continued to deal with Adam and Eve and their offspring at certain set times at the east entrance of the garden.

In the Old Testament, only the named patriarchs were chosen by God to receive an opportunity for salvation and be in the first resurrection at Christ's return. Salvation offered under the New Covenant will be discussed starting in Chapter 7.

5. J. P. Green, *The Interlinear Hebrew-Greek-English Bible*

CHAPTER FOUR

God Continues to Create Through
Human Procreation

In God's initial creation of all life forms, He fashioned within them the ability to reproduce after their *own kind* (Gen. 1:20-25). He created all animals as male and female—as He did human life. Accordingly, they are able to *procreate*—produce offspring after *their kind*. It is the same with flora. Through seeds, plant life is reproduced after its kind. Thus, while God upholds and controls the universe and the earth, He continues the miracle of *creating life*. Whether human, mammal, reptile, fish, fowl or plant, God's creation of life continues through various means of *procreation*.

Throughout God's creation, we find similarity of design—all pointing to a single Creator. But we also find tremendous diversity and uniqueness. Every grain of sand, every pebble or stone, every snowflake—each is similar, but unique. An entire forest of maple trees has the same overall pattern and color, yet each tree—even each leaf—is unique.

It is the same with animal life: There are classes and genera of life incorporating various species, yet each individual creature within a species has its own unique genetic identity—and this uniqueness removes the possibility of having exact duplicates. This *uniqueness* found within a broad *similarity* of design is absolute evidence that evolution's "random selection" could never have produced what we see throughout the universe, the earth, and within all life!

Most importantly, this uniqueness is a prominent feature of human life. God created within Adam and Eve the genetics necessary for the production of all the various races.

Human Life Continues—In Spite of Sin

When Adam and Eve sinned against God—and believed the serpent's lie that they could decide for themselves what was good and what was evil—they actually placed themselves under the authority of Satan the devil. Thus, Lucifer became the "god" of this world. While the true God has maintained His overall sovereignty, He has allowed mankind to go its own way. Only the pre-Flood patriarchs listed in Genesis five believed God and were counted as righteous.

Genesis four relates a summary of the line of Cain. Cain and all of his descendants, as well as the unrighteous ones of Seth's line, followed and worshiped Satan. Thus, the whole world became filled with violence, corruption, wickedness and evil. God's judgment was to destroy mankind with the Great Flood. But to preserve the human family, as well as the animals, God instructed Noah to build an ark to carry him, his family, and the animals through the flood. God saved only *eight* people—Noah, his wife, their three sons, and their wives. [1]

After the flood mankind again increased in number—and soon returned to serving Satan, false gods and idols.

In spite of mankind's sinful behavior, the *process of human procreation* has continued exactly as God intended. Indeed, God has continued to display His *creative power* in the numerous miracles involved in the procreation of new human life. Moreover, the procreation of human life will continue until the end of this *present phase* of God's plan.

In His mercy, God has again filled the earth with people, having formed them into various families, tribes and nations. The Word of God proclaims that *He* has made them all: "**All nations whom You have made**…" (Psa. 86:9). The apostle Paul writes, "And He made of one blood **all the nations of men** to dwell upon all the face of the earth, having determined beforehand *their* appointed times and the boundaries of their dwelling" (Acts 17:26).

In the future, after Jesus Christ returns to the earth as King and Savior of the world, this Psalm will be fulfilled: "Shout for joy to the LORD, all the earth. Serve the LORD with gladness; come before His presence with singing. Know that the LORD, He is God. **He has made us**, **and we are His**; we are His people and the sheep of His pasture" (Psa. 100:1-3).

Yet because of the almost infinite combination of genes and chromosomes, the genetic code of every human being is unique. Though all human beings, male and female, are made in the image of God (according to the "God kind"), there are no two individuals exactly alike—not even so-called "identical twins"!

What Scientists Have Discovered About Human Genetics

The discovery of genes and chromosomes was a landmark event in science. However, it was not until 1990 that scientists began to "map" the human genome—to catalog every gene in the human body. In fact, advanced genetic research has given scientists a look at just how intricate God has made man and woman—particularly in the area of human reproduction.

But because scientists ignore the Bible, they could not know of one of the most important aspects of human makeup—the *spirit of man*. This means they are unaware of the *power* God actually uses in creating human beings in the womb. Indeed, such ignorance only helps to keep scientists in the dark concerning God's purpose for mankind.

The presence of this unique *spirit* in humans explains why genetics alone cannot account for human personality and behavior. In her book concerning genetics, *How to Reprogram Your DNA for Optimum Health,* Adelle LaBrec writes:

"Many scientists predicted that the success of the [human genome] project would radically reconfigure not only the world of medicine, but the world as we know it. Once the estimated 25,000 [to 100,000] genes that make up human DNA had been sequenced, we would have unlocked the genetic key to how we look, feel, think, and behave. With the human genome map in hand, many scientists believed that there would quite literally be no more mysteries about human life. As Jean-Pierre Issa, professor of microbiology at Temple University, puts it, 'When the human genome was sequenced, some scientists were saying, "That's the end. We're going to understand every disease. We're going to understand every behavior" ' " [2]

LaBrec continues: "However, when the Human Genome Project finally concluded in March of 2000, it quickly became clear that these hopes had been overly optimistic to some degree.... [A] piece of the puzzle was still missing. And it was a critical piece with respect to providing a full and complete view of human health and the role of genes in the development of disease. 'As it turns out,' Issa notes, the picture was incomplete because 'the sequence of DNA isn't enough to explain behavior. It isn't enough to explain the diseases.'

"In the decade since, scientists have discovered that genes tell only part of the story. The rest is written in epigenetics—alterations to the way that genetic traits are expressed. These epigenetic alterations do not change the DNA sequence itself, but they are extremely influential nevertheless." [3]

"Before delving into the world of epigenetics, a quick review of genetics is in order. As the word 'epigenetics' itself indicates, the two subjects are inextricably enmeshed. Each cell in your body is formed from 46 chromosomes, 23 from the mother's egg and 23 from the father's sperm. These chromosomes contain 60,000 to 100,000 genes in the form of *deoxyribonucleic acid*, a complex molecule commonly known as DNA. As the primary hereditary unit for all living things, DNA contains the information needed to build and maintain a living organism.

"Your DNA provides the raw material for your physical appearance and personality. When your cells duplicate, they pass this genetic information on to the newly formed cells. These immature cells are known as stem cells, and stem cells have the potential to become any type of fully differentiated adult cells. All of your cells—from those making up the nail on your pinky finger to those forming the innermost chamber of your heart—have an identical DNA blueprint, regardless of how completely different the functions [of] each cell ... may be." [4]

"Ultimately, your genes carry the instructions that not only first allowed your body (and every organ, tissue, and cell) to develop, but that also now allow your body to create all the things it needs to function. Those functions are set by your epigenes, which instruct fetal cells to develop according to their intended roles. Until recently scientists believed that cellular function was 'set' during gestation, but it has now been shown that epigenes are actively involved in cell function over the entire course of a person's life." [5]

Going beyond the structure and function of individual cells, quantum physics is the study of the universe and all living things on a *subatomic* level: "One of the most empowering aspects of quantum physics is that the universe is fluid and always changing. In fact, what quantum physics teaches us is that the universe is renewed on a subatomic level every few seconds....

"On a subatomic level, everything in our lives—external and internal—is refreshed and renewed every trillionth of a second or so. Therefore, by the laws of quantum physics, every moment is literally a new beginning.

"Dr. Bruce Lipton's work reflects a deep respect for and understanding of these laws of quantum physics. His breakthrough studies revealed that epigenes, located on the cell [outer] membrane, transmit electromagnetic signals to the interior of the cells. These signals are produced by our senses, thoughts, beliefs, and emotions. Just as you mentally adjust to your environment, so, too, your cells respond to their environment.

"Dr. Lipton compared the outer layer of the cell—the epigene—to a computer chip. If your DNA is your genetic hardware, your epigenes are your software. Research conducted by Dr. Lipton between 1987 and 1992 showed that the epigene conveys information about environmental factors that control the behavior and physiology of the [individual] cell.... In his two major publications discussing his discoveries, Dr. Lipton explained how molecular pathways connect the mind and body, and more importantly, how retraining our thinking can change our bodies. This is both inspiring and motivating, because if we can change our cells by changing our minds, our lives are not completely controlled by our DNA." [6]

Cutting-edge bio-molecular science gives us great insight into the complexity of human life, especially concerning how our bodies and minds function. However, because the *spirit of man* is invisible, science remains ignorant of this unique *power* from God that actually facilitates the creation of human life in the womb and that sustains one's life until death—as "the body is dead without the spirit" (James 2:26).

The Spirit of Man in Human Procreation

The Bible affirms that even those of ancient times had some knowledge of the *spirit of man*—the spirit that God gives to each human at conception. They understood that it was this *spirit* that actually brought about the creation of life in the womb. When speaking to the patriarch Job, the young Elihu said, "**The Spirit of God has made me, and the breath of the Almighty gives me life**" (Job 33:4). Elihu was referring to the fact that it was God Who made and formed him in his mother's womb by His Spirit (Zech. 12:1). The prophet Isaiah refers to God as the one who "created the heavens and stretched them out, spreading forth the earth"—who "**gives breath to the people upon it and spirit to those who walk in it**" (Isa. 42:5).

Without a doubt, it is the *spirit of man* that imparts godlike attributes to humans. It makes it possible for us to *think* and *reason*. Paul writes, "For who among men understands the things of man **except *by* the spirit of man which *is* in him**? (I Cor. 2:11). This confirms Elihu's declaration, "But *there is* **a spirit in man and the inspiration of the Almighty gives them understanding**" (Job 32:8).

King David praised God for the knowledge that *He* is the one who *creates life* in the womb. He understood that procreation occurs according to a set order or pattern: "**I will praise You, for I am awesomely and wonderfully made**; Your works are marvelous and my soul knows it very well. My **substance** was not hidden from You when **I was made in secret and intricately formed** in the lowest parts of the earth [symbolic of the womb]. Your eyes did see my **substance, yet being unformed; and in Your book all my members were written, which in continuance were fashioned, when as yet there were none of them**" (Psa. 139:14-16).

Today, the scientific name for newly conceived life, yet unformed, is still "substance." The "members" written in God's "book" of procreation are now called the "human genome." By the power of God's Spirit working through the *spirit of man,* all the "members" or parts of a newly conceived infant are fashioned throughout its nine months in the womb. The growing baby is the combined *genetic expression* of his or her father and mother. Moreover, every human being has ultimately descended from the *original* genes that God created in Adam and Eve. Thus, David proclaimed to God, "**Your hands have made me and formed me**" (Psa. 119:73).

This statement is true because God created the *original* genes and chromosomes in Adam and Eve—containing within them an almost infinite variety of human characteristics—from which all mankind would be produced through procreation. Thus, all human beings down through time have been formed by God.

God explained this to the prophet Jeremiah: "And it came to pass, the Word of the Lord came to me, saying, '**Before I formed you in the belly I knew you** [this means God knew Jeremiah at the *instant* of his conception]; and before you came forth out of the womb I consecrated you, *and* I ordained you a prophet to the nations" (Jer. 1:4-5).

Indeed, each individual is *unique*; each newly begotten baby is a *special creation*, being "made and formed" by God. In human procreation, it is the father who begets the new human life in the womb of the mother. This begettal takes place when a sperm from the father penetrates the ovum of the mother and conception occurs. It is at this precise instant that God gives the *spirit of man* and a new human being is conceived. Jesus said, "It is the Spirit that gives life" (John 6:63).

Infused with the power of the *spirit of man*, the combined genetic material from the father and the mother of the newly conceived infant begins to develop immediately. Without the *spirit of man* there can be no human life. Since the *spirit of man* is invisible, science remains ignorant of this unique *power* from God that actually facilitates the creation of human life in the womb and that sustains one's life until death—as "the body is dead without the spirit" (James 2:26).

At this instant of conception, a *miracle* takes place. In his book *Young Again*, John Thomas describes this "bio-electric/spirit" event:

"Human sperm makes the long trip into the woman's fallopian tubes to fertilize the ovum with power generated by the mitochondria. The base of the sperm's tail is heavily laden with mitochondria. When sperm fertilizes the egg (ovum), the electrical discharge of 480,000 volts of electricity comes from both the sperm and the ovum. Both are 'energy' bodies—one is HUGE, the other is miniscule....

"The electrical discharge the ovum generates is only 0.19 volts. The discharge by the sperm is 25,263,157 times GREATER than that of the ovum—a huge difference! There is a massive difference in physical size between the sperm and ovum. The volume of the ovum is $1,760,000^3$ microns; and the sperm 21^3 microns. When we divide the size of the ovum by the size of the sperm, we find that the egg is 83,809 times GREATER! These differences in physical size and electrical potential generate the release of the 480,000 volts called *bio-electric lightning!*" [7]

Thomas continues: "The electric 'discharge' coagulates [and seals] the ovum's outer surface, preventing penetration by other sperm. This massive electrical event is the beginning of a new 'life!' Death is a similar—but opposite—electrical event where 'spirit' energy exits the body and returns from whence it came." [8]

At the instant of conception, when this "bio-electric discharge" takes place, *God gives the spirit of man*—thus creating the beginning of a new human life. While this discharge can be detected by specialized instruments, it is invisible. It is the *spirit of man* from God that empowers the combined genes and chromosomes from the father [9] and the mother [10] to begin developing a new human life according to the sequence God has designed. Thus, it takes *three* components to create each new human being: First, the *sperm* from the father; second, the *ovum* from the mother; and third, the *spirit of man* from God.

Though this new life is only the size of a microscopic speck of dust, it is still a *unique human life*. It already contains all of the genetic information it will ever need; all that is required is the *time* it takes to develop in the womb, to have a live birth, and then grow into an adult.

During the baby's formation in the womb, as soon as its heart begins to function, it begins to partake of the "breath of life" through the transfer of oxygen from the blood of the mother, through the placenta and umbilical cord, into the blood of the infant.

Using advanced imaging technology, doctors can take 3-D pictures of developing infants in the womb. Indeed, we can now *witness* the entire miraculous process—from conception to birth! While in the womb, the new baby boy or girl lives in a watery environment. Once born, however, the infant's environment suddenly changes. The birthing process involves a rapidly-occurring series of miracles on the part of the mother and the baby, all of which must be perfectly timed and sequenced in order to have a successful delivery.

The following pages feature extraordinary images of God's actual *creation* of new human life in the womb through procreation!

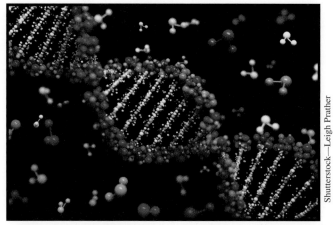

Genetic Chromosome Helix

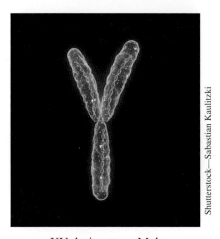

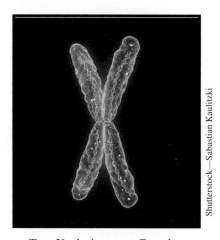

XY designates a Male   Two Xs designates a Female

Each person at conception receives 23 chromosomes from the father and 23 from the mother, for a total of 46 chromosomes. The chromosome that *determines sex* comes from the father. The male chromosome is designated the Y chromosome; the female chromosome is called the X chromosome. While the father produces *both* Y and X chromosomes, each sperm cell will carry only one Y *or* one X chromosome. The mother produces only the X chromosome, and each ovum contains only one. When a sperm cell carrying the Y chromosome impregnates the mother, the infant will be a boy. This is why a male is genetically designated as XY. When a sperm cell carrying the X chromosome impregnates the mother, the infant will be a girl. Thus, the female is designated as XX.

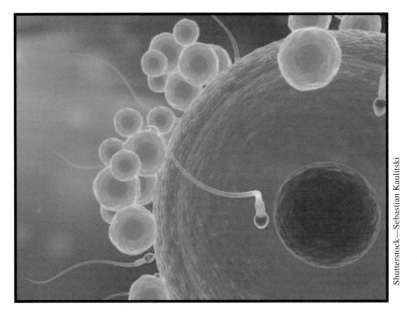

The sperm from the father begets a new life in the egg of the mother.

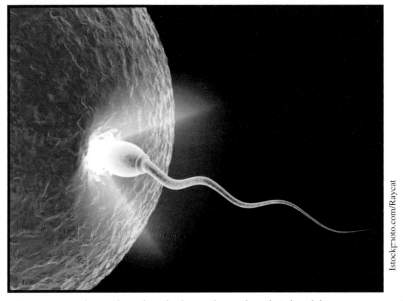

At conception, the size is less than the dot in this square, and that is the *beginning of human life!* As full grown adults, we are trillions of times larger.

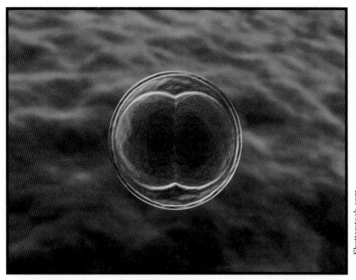

The first division of new human cells, which takes place right after conception.

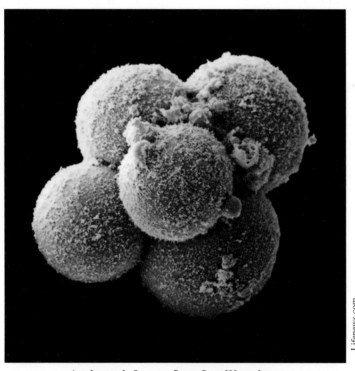

At just 4 days after fertilization...

What? That zygote doesn't look human? Well, not yet! It's growing, so it must be alive. It has human parents, so it must be human. In fact, that zygote is a girl! And she has her own unique set of human DNA. Her DNA will guide her body's development over the next nine months—and over her entire lifetime!

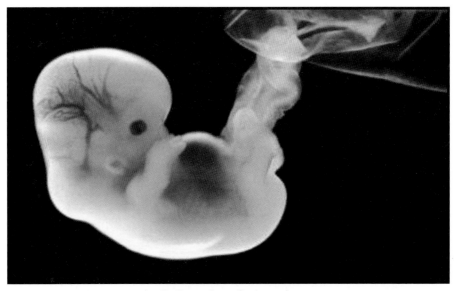

At 5-6 weeks of gestation...

Despite being only a quarter of an inch long, her nose, mouth, and ears are already taking shape! Her heart is beating about 100 times a minute (almost twice as fast as yours) and blood is beginning to circulate through her body. Brain waves have been detectable for at least 2-3 weeks already!

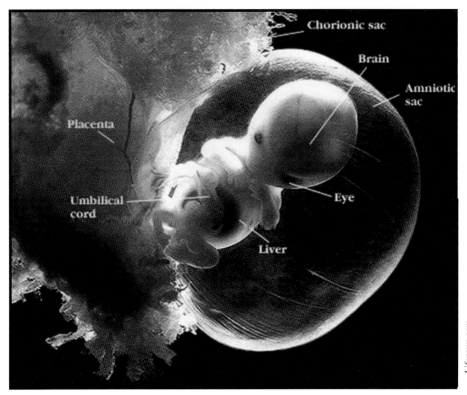

At just 7 weeks gestation...

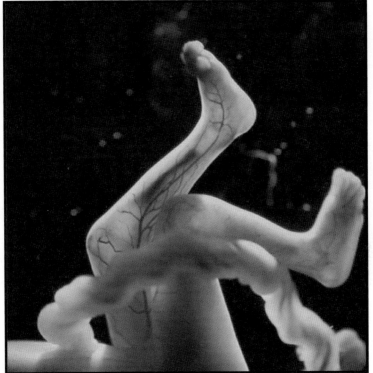

Lifenews.com

At about 10 weeks...

All of her major body functions are up and running: the kidneys, intestines, brain, and liver are all working. Her tiny arms and legs can already start to flex. Most abortions in the United States take place around this time. If she is lucky, her mom will love her enough to let her live.

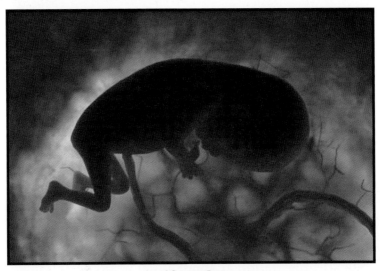

Lifenews.com

At 12 weeks...

Her muscles are beginning to bulk up, so she's busily stretching and kicking. If you put your hand on your tummy, she'll likely wiggle in response (although you won't feel it yet) because her reflexes are starting to develop.

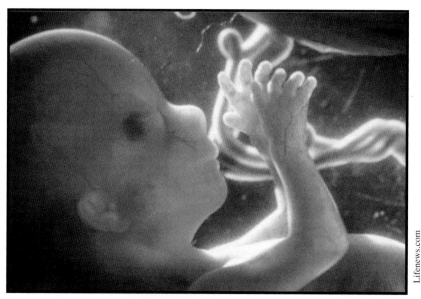

At 16 weeks gestation...

This week, the baby is going through a growth spurt. Soon she'll be growing locks of hair on her head and she's already started growing toenails. Her heart pumps about 25 quarts of blood through her body every day!

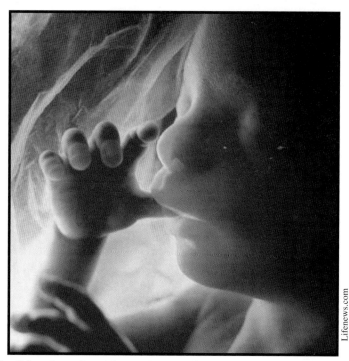

Sucking her thumb at about 18-20 weeks gestation...

Right about now she has her own unique set of fingerprints.

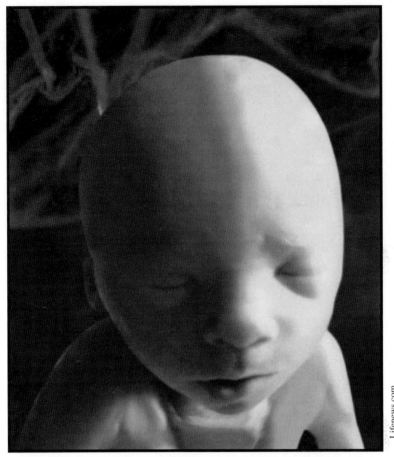

At 6 months gestation…

The baby can now respond to external sounds by moving and increasing the pulse. A mother may notice jerking motions if the baby hiccups!

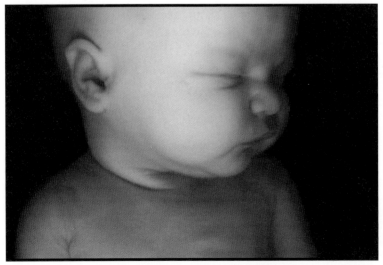

Around 6-7 months gestation…

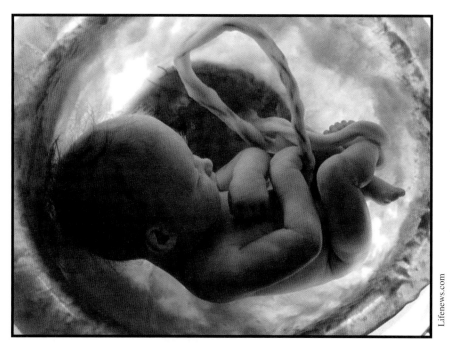

Lifenews.com

At around 8 months gestation...

This baby can hear and is beginning to recognize her mother's voice. Her skin is pink and she is already beginning to get that cute, chunky appearance that newborns have. That extra fat is very important because it allows the baby to regulate her temperature after birth.

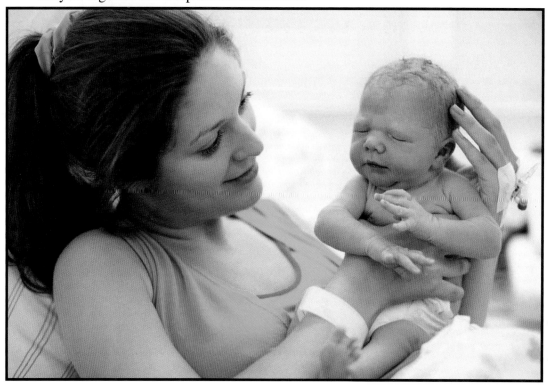

shutterstock.com

The Wait and the Reward
Artwork by Anna Rose Bain
Original painting size 30X30 inches, oil on linen
Self portrait begun when artist was 34 weeks pregnant and
completed when her daughter was two weeks old.
Used with permission by the artist, www.artworkbyannarose.com

Shutterstock—ZouZou

Shutterstock—ffoto29

Shutterstock—Marino bocelli

God Continues to Create Through Human Procreation

Shutterstock—Anneka

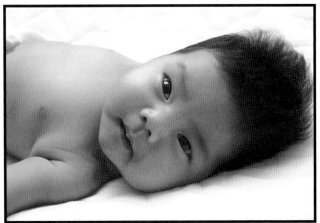

Shutterstock—komnphoto

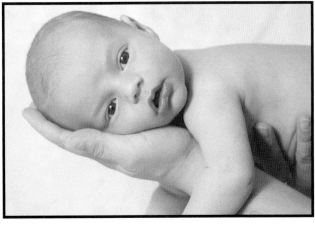

Shutterstock—margo_black

Shutterstock—Anton_Ivanov

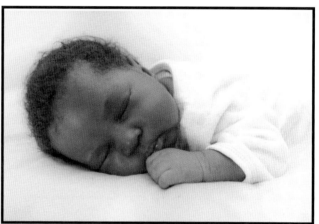

Shutterstock—Tatiana Katsai

iStockphoto.com/vanentimrussanov

The Glory of the Sand of the Sea

When God confirmed His covenant promises to Abraham, He declared that his physical descendants would be as *"the sand of the sea"* (Gen. 22:17). Later, King David wrote this concerning God's creation of man and woman: "You have made him a little lower than God and have *crowned him with glory and honor*." The following pictures of grains of sand, magnified 250 times, reveal that even ordinary grains of sand contain a hidden beauty and glory that is symbolic of human "glory and honor," which God created in mankind.

The tip of a spiral shell has broken off and become a grain of sand. After being repeatedly tumbled by the action of the surf, this spiral sand grain has become opalescent in character. It is surrounded by bits of coral, a pink shell fragment, a foram (a type of protozoa), and volcanic material. Photo copyright Dr. Gary Greenberg. www.sandgrains.com

The glacially deposited sands around Lake Winnibigoshish, Minnesota, contain abundant sediments from the igneous and metamorphic minerals of the Lake Superior basin. A sample includes pink garnets, green epidote, iron-rich red agates, black magnetite, and hematite. Image Copyright 2008 Dr. Gary Greenberg. www.sandgrains.com

A handful of sand grains selected from a beach in Maui and arranged on a black background. Photo copyright Dr. Gary Greenberg. www.sandgrains.com

Every grain of sand is a jewel waiting to be discovered. That's what Dr. Gary Greenberg found when he first turned his microscope on the beach sand. Gemlike minerals, colorful coral fragments, and delicate microscopic shells reveal that sand comprises much more than tiny beige rocks. www.sandgrains.com

Many grains of sand are tiny crystals (shiny, flat sided solids). Sand from Zushi Beach, Japan, contains what looks like a sapphire crystal. The crystal is larger than the surrounding grains and has survived eroding because of its hardness and quality. Image Copyright 2008 Dr. Gary Greenberg. www.sandgrains.com

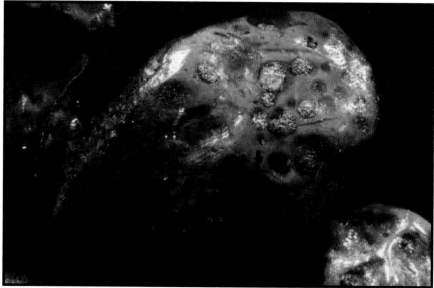

MAKENA BLACK & RED
Glassy red and black volcanic sand grains are found in the sand from Makena Point, Hawaii. Image copyright Dr. Gary Greenburg. www.sandgrains.com

Chapter 4 Notes:

1. "And the LORD saw that the wickedness of man *was* great on the earth, and every imagination of the thoughts of his heart *was* only evil continually. And the LORD repented that He had made man on the earth, and He *was* grieved in His heart. And the LORD said, 'I will destroy man whom I have created from the face of the earth, both man and beast, and the crawling thing, and the fowl of the air; for I repent that I have made them.'

"But Noah found grace in the eyes of the LORD. These *are* the generations of Noah. Noah was a righteous man and perfect in his generations, for Noah walked with God. And Noah begat three sons: Shem, Ham, and Japheth.

"Now the earth also was corrupt before God, and the earth was filled with violence. And God looked upon the earth, and behold, it was corrupt— for all flesh had corrupted its way upon the earth. And God said to Noah, 'The end of all flesh has come before Me, for the earth is filled with violence through them. And, behold, I will destroy them *with* the earth' " (Gen. 6:5-13).

2. Adelle LaBrec, *How to Reprogram Your DNA for Optimum Health*; Think-Outside-the-Book Publishing, Beverly Hills, Calif. 2014; p.1

3. *Ibid*, p .2

4. *Ibid*, pp. 8-9

5. *Ibid*, p. 9

6. *Ibid*, pp. 12-13

7. John Thomas, *Young Again! How to Reverse the Aging Process*; Plexus Press, Mead, Wash. 2006; pp. 255-256

8. *Ibid*, p. 252

9. *Facts about male sperm:* From puberty, males continually produce sperm. The average man will produce roughly 525 billion sperm cells over his reproductive lifetime—and will shed at least 1 billion of them per month (www.scienceline.org; June 2008).

10. *Facts about female eggs (ovum):* Women are born with an average of two million egg follicles, the reproductive structures that give rise to eggs. By puberty, a majority of those follicles will have closed up and only about 450 will ever release mature eggs for potential fertilization (www.scienceline.org; June 2008)

Throughout a woman's reproductive life, the vast majority of follicles will expire through a process known as *atresia*, which actually begins at birth. When a woman reaches puberty and starts to menstruate, only about 400,000 follicles remain. With each menstrual cycle a thousand follicles are lost, and only one lucky little follicle will actually mature into an ovum (egg), which is released into the fallopian tube, kicking off ovulation. This means that of the one to two million follicles present at birth, only about 400 will ever mature (Go Ask Alice; www.columbia.edu).

During fetal life, there are about 6 to 7 million eggs. From this time no new eggs are produced. At birth, there are approximately 1 million eggs; and by the time of puberty, only about 300,000 remain. Of these, only 300 to 400 will be ovulated during a woman's reproductive lifetime (www.clevelandclinic.org).

By the time a woman is 30, nearly all of her ovarian eggs are gone for good. According to a study published by the University of St. Andrews and Edinburgh University in Scotland, women who put off childbearing for too long could have difficulty conceiving. The study found that women have lost 90 percent of their eggs by the time they are 30, and only have about 3 percent remaining by the time they are 40 (ABC News; Jan. 29, 2010).

11. Abortion is murder: Each newly conceived human being is only the size of a microscopic speck of dust, yet it is still a *unique human life*. It already contains all of the genetic information it will ever need; all that is required is the *time* it takes to develop in the womb, to have a live birth, and then grow into an adult. **Thus, we have absolute proof from the Word of God and from modern science that human *life begins at conception*. Therefore, abortion is the *murder* of a human being!**

Did You Know?...

There are miracles going on in our bodies every day. As we age, we may feel like our body is beginning to creak and fail us on the outside, but consider the incredible work that is taking place inside of it. There is so much going on and everything fits together so well, that it is almost impossible to comprehend it, all of which proves that they had to be created by God.

Your heart pumps approximately 2000 gallons (7571 liter) of blood through its chambers every single day. It beats more than 100,000 times a day to achieve this incredible feat.

You take around 17,000 breaths a day on average, and don't have to think about a single one of them. A typical pair of adult lungs can hold a huge six liters of air.

Every day your body ensures you don't contract cancer thousands of times over. Cancer is formed when cells are altered in a way which reprograms their DNA and it's estimated that tens of thousands of cells suffer cancer-causing lesions every day. But the body sends special enzymes scuttling around to inspect DNA strands for faults and fix them before they turn into tumors.

Your brain doesn't stop working. It's estimated that about 50,000-60,000 thoughts pass through it each day. That is a whopping 35-48 thoughts every minute.

The cells in your stomach lining produce an alkaline substance every few milliseconds to neutralize stomach acid. If they didn't do this, your stomach would digest itself because some of the acids are strong enough to dissolve metals.

You blink your eyes about 28,800 times every day, with each one lasting just a tenth of a second. This is a voluntary reflex the body uses to keep the eyes clean and moist, which is pretty crucial given that 90% of the information you process is visual.

Most of the body's energy is expelled via heat. Your body produces the same heat as 25 light bulbs over the course of a single day.

Red blood cells literally shoot around the body, taking less than 60 seconds to complete a full circuit. This means that each of yours makes 1400 trips around your body every day, delivering oxygen and keeping your body energized. Each cell lives for about 40 days, making 60,000 trips around the body!

Your liver manufactures cholesterol, vitamin D & blood plasma; it identi-

Did You Know?...

fies the nutrients your body needs, and stores some away for future use; it filters 1.53 quarts (1.43 liters) of blood every minute and produces a quart (0.94 liters) of bile every day to help you break down your food.

You shed more than 1 million skin cells every single day but they are constantly replenished automatically. Your skin is actually the largest organ you have, with a surface area of 18 square feet (2 square meters).

Your hair grows about half a millimeter per day, and the average adult with a full scalp has around 100,000 hairs on their head. So that is a combined 50 meters of hair growth every single day.

The brain and mouth work together to allow us to speak an average of around 5000 words a day. Some studies suggest men average about 2000 words per day but only about 500-700 of those words uttered by either sex is useful information.

The glands in your mouth produce 1-5 liters of saliva every day.

Each of your kidneys contain 1 million tiny filters that work together to filter an average of 2.2 pints of blood every minute—that's 3168 pints (1872 liters) every single day, despite each kidney being only the size of a fist. If that wasn't enough, they also expel an average of 2.5 pints (1.4 liters) of urine from your body every day also.

You grow 8mm every night while sleeping, before shrinking back down again the next day. This saves you from some pretty hefty clothing bills and ensures you don't have to raise the door frames every year or two.

Your body works overtime to digest your food and the process starts before it even hits your mouth. When you smell food, your mouth automatically produces more saliva to prepare the digestive system for work. It takes about 6-8 hours for food to pass through the stomach and two days to complete the digestion process. The average person will eat over 50 tons of food in his or her lifetime, which seems ridiculous!

And most amazing of all, your body cells are regenerating themselves every single day without any prompting. This means you have an entirely new set of taste buds every ten days, new nails every 6-10 months, new bones every 10 years and even a new heart every 20 years.

CHAPTER FIVE

God's Covenant with Abraham

After the Flood in 2369 BC, God made a *covenant* with Noah and his sons and all the earth to never again flood the world and destroy all life (Gen. 9:1-17). The perpetual sign of that covenant promise is the rainbow. Noah lived an additional 350 years after the Flood. However, approximately 50 years before his death, Satan again persuaded the majority of mankind to rebel against God's rule. The devil's human leader, the tyrannical Nimrod, proclaimed himself to be God's replacement (Gen. 10:8-11). He introduced idolatry, sun worship, and even the worship of Satan. In fact, Nimrod's idolatrous teachings and practices feature prominently in the religions of today's world,[1] and the apostle Paul described Nimrod's religion as the "mystery" of lawlessness and iniquity (II Thes. 2:7).

In their defiance against God, Nimrod's followers united and began to build the tower of Babel: "And they said, 'Come, let us build us a city and a tower, *with* its top reaching into the heavens. And let us establish a name for ourselves, lest we be scattered upon the face of the whole earth.' And the LORD came down to see the city and the tower which the children of men had built. And the LORD said, 'Behold, the people *are* one and they all have one language. And this *is only the beginning of* what they will do—now nothing which they have imagined to do will be restrained from them. Come, let Us go down and there confuse their language, so that they cannot understand one another's speech.' So the LORD scattered them abroad from that place upon the face of all the earth. And they quit building the city. Therefore the name of it is called Babel, because the LORD confused the language of all the earth there. And from there the LORD scattered them abroad upon the face of all the earth" (Gen. 11:4-9).

God's Covenantal Promises to Abraham

Approximately 430 years after the Flood, God called Abram when he was 75 years old and commanded him to leave the idolatrous Babylonian city of Ur of the Chaldees: "And the LORD said to Abram, 'Get out of your country, and from your kindred, and from your father's house into a land that I will show you. **And I will make *of* you a great nation. And I will bless you and make your name great. And you shall be a blessing. And I**

will bless those that bless you and curse the one who curses you. And in you shall all families of the earth be blessed.' Then Abram departed, even as the LORD had spoken to him" (Gen. 12:1-4).

Few realize that God's entire plan for mankind, including man's astounding destiny, is an outgrowth of God's *promises* to Abram. Indeed, God's promises to Abram would ultimately affect "*all families of the earth*"—meaning every single person—past, present and future! So awesome are God's promises, and His covenant He established with Abram, that **they are the foundation and the reason for the rest of the entire Bible!** (God later renamed him Abraham, meaning the "father of many nations.")

In addition, these Abrahamic promises reach back and are connected to God's promise to Adam and Eve in Genesis 3:15 of the coming Messiah—the Savior of the world. As Creator of the heavens and the earth and of life itself, **the LORD GOD ALMIGHTY has the power to fulfill every prophecy and promise He makes!** Each promise or prophecy concerning man's glorious destiny are like pages in a book—which, when turned page by page, reveal various aspects of God's plan for mankind. Because of the sin of Adam and Eve, God has kept this plan *secret* "from the foundation of the world" (Matt. 13:35).

God's covenant with Abraham contained *two major promises*. The **first promise** concerned *physical seed* through Abraham's own son, Isaac: "And the Word of the LORD came to [Abraham] saying ... '[He] that shall come forth out of your own loins shall be your heir' " (Gen. 15:4). Along with the promise of physical seed was the promise of land—the Promised Land—a physical kingdom.

Those who study the Bible realize that the fulfillment of the first promise came through Isaac—then through Isaac's son, Jacob, who was the father of the twelve tribes of Israel. Much of the Old Testament contains the histories and future prophecies of Israel and Judah—the descendants of the promised physical seed, a multitude of nations and kings (Gen. 17:1-21). [2]

Moreover, the prophesied Messiah—who would come 1925 years after God's covenant with Abraham—was of the physical seed of David, of the tribe of Judah. The Gospel of Matthew records: "*The* book of *the* genealogy of Jesus Christ, *the* son of David, *the* son of Abraham: Abraham begat Isaac; and Isaac begat Jacob; and Jacob begat Judah and his brethren [the other eleven tribes of Israel]" (Matt. 1:1-2).

Jesus had *preexisted* as God before He became human—"God manifested in the flesh" (Phil. 2:6-8; I Tim. 3:16). (This will be fully explained in Chapter Seven.) The Messiah had to come in the *flesh*, as this prophecy in Isaiah reveals: "**For unto us a Child is born**, unto us a son is given; and the government shall be upon His shoulder; and His name shall be called Wonderful, Counselor, **The Mighty God**, The Everlasting Father, The Prince of Peace. Of the increase of *His* government and peace *there shall be* no end, upon the throne of David, and over His kingdom, to order it and to establish it with judgment and with righteousness from henceforth, even forever. The zeal of the LORD of hosts will do this" (Isa. 9:6-7). [3] As we will see, all of the above is connected to promise number two.

The **second promise** concerned *spiritual seed*. "And [God] brought [Abraham] outside and said, '**Look now toward the heavens and number the stars—if you are able to count them.**' **And He said to him, 'So shall your seed be.'** And he believed in the LORD. And He accounted it to him for righteousness" (Gen. 15:5-6).

God told Abraham to look to the heavens and *count* the stars—an impossibility! Why would God compare Abraham's descendants with the stars? As another page is turned in the book of the "mystery of God," we will see that the heavens are an allusion of *eternity* and the stars symbolize eternal *glory*. The prophet Daniel reveals the interpretation of God's reference to the heavens and the stars when he writes of the time of the end and of the glory of the *first* resurrection: "And there shall be a time of trouble, such as never was since there was a nation even until that time [the time of the end]. And at that time your people shall be delivered—every one who shall be found written in the book. **And many of those who sleep in the dust of the earth shall awake, some to everlasting life**, and some to shame and everlasting contempt. **And they who are wise shall shine as the brightness of the firmament, and they who turn many to righteousness shall shine as the stars forever and ever**" (Dan. 12:1-3).

Although Daniel's words help us to understand God's second promise to Abraham, the full meaning of the first resurrection, when Jesus returns, could not be understood until the time of the New Testament—the teachings of Christ and the inspired writings of His chosen apostles.

We can get another glimpse of this revelation from the apostle Paul. In speaking of the first resurrection of the dead to eternal life, he adds to the meaning and interpretation of God's promises to Abraham—*first*, physical seed; *second*, spiritual seed. Paul writes: "However, the spiritual *was* not first, but **the natural—then the spiritual**. The first man [Adam] *is* of the earth—made of dust. The second Man [Jesus the Messiah] *is* the Lord from heaven" (I Cor. 15:46-47). This is the same sequence of God's promises to Abraham—the physical seed *first*, the spiritual seed *second*.

With Daniel's and Paul's explanation, we are able to perceive quite clearly that God's second promise to Abraham—the heavens and the stars— is a symbolic allusion to *the spiritual seed*. Thus, the second promise is the *greater* promise. However, in accord with what Paul wrote, the promised *spiritual seed* can only come from among those who were first of the *physical seed*—human beings—of "all families of the earth." Indeed, humans are *first* made of the dust of the earth, through procreation; but ultimately, through the resurrection, they are made *spirit* beings.

The Covenant Promises Sealed Through Two Special Sacrifices

There were two special sacrifices that were made to ratify God's two covenant promises to Abraham—promises of physical seed and of spiritual seed. The *first covenant sacrifice* was sealed and ratified by God Himself with a special maledictory oath and unique animal sacrifices (Gen. 15:9-18).[4] God instructed Abraham to prepare three animals—splitting them into two halves, from head to tail—and make a path between the parts. To ratify His covenant with Abraham, God *alone* walked between the halves of the sacrificial animals. By doing so, God essentially pledged *His own future death* as a guarantee that He would fulfill the covenant promises. Abraham, however, did *not* walk between the parts of the animals.

Then, 30 years later, God required a *second* special covenant sacrifice, when Abraham was 115 years old and Isaac was 15 years old.[5] Both Abraham and Isaac were directly involved in this second covenant sacrifice. It is important to read this entire account because it contains so much meaning:

"And it came to pass after these things that God tested Abraham, and said to him, 'Abraham!' And he said, 'Here I am.' And He said, '**Take now your son, your only** *son* **Isaac, whom you love, and go into the land of Moriah, and offer him there for a burnt offering upon one of the mountains which I will tell you**.'

"And Abraham rose up early in the morning and saddled his donkey, and took two *of* his young men with him, and Isaac his son. And he split the wood for the burnt offering, and rose up and went to the place of which God had told him. Then on the third day Abraham lifted up his eyes and saw the place afar off.

"And Abraham said to his young men, 'You stay here with the donkey, and I and the boy will go yonder and worship, and come again to you.' And **Abraham took the wood of the burnt offering and laid it upon Isaac his son**. And he took the fire *pot* in his hand, and a knife. And they both went together. And Isaac spoke to Abraham his father and said, 'My father.' And he said, 'Here I *am*, my son.' And he said, 'Behold the fire and the wood. But where is the lamb for a burnt offering?' And Abraham said, '**My son, God will provide Himself a lamb for a burnt offering**.' So they both went on together. And they came to the place of which God had told him. And Abraham built an altar there and laid the wood in order. **And he bound his son Isaac and laid him on the wood, upon the altar**. **And Abraham stretched out his hand and took the knife to slay his son.**

"And the angel of the LORD called to him from the heavens and said, 'Abraham! Abraham!' And he said, 'Here I *am*.' And He said, '**Do not lay your hand upon the lad, nor do anything to him, for now I know that you fear God, seeing you have not withheld your son, your only son, from Me**.' **And Abraham lifted up his eyes and looked. And, behold, behind** *him* **a ram was entangled in a thicket by its horns. And Abraham went and took the ram and offered it up for a burnt offering instead of his son**. And Abraham called the name of that place The LORD Will Provide; so that it is said *until* this day, 'In the mount of the LORD it will be provided.'

"And the angel of the LORD called to Abraham out of heaven the second time, and said, '**By Myself have I sworn**,' says the LORD, '**because you have done this thing, and have not withheld your son, your only son; that in blessing I will bless you, and in multiplying I will multiply your seed like the stars of the heavens** [the spiritual seed—the children of God]**, and as the sand which is upon the seashore.** And your seed [physical seed—the children of Israel] shall possess the gate of his enemies. **And in your Seed** [Jesus Christ, Gal. 3:14-16] **shall all the nations of the earth be blessed, because you have obeyed My voice**' " (Gen. 22:1-18).

While this was a literal covenant sacrifice, there is a great deal of prophetic-spiritual meaning relating to the Messiah's death. Let us examine the spiritual symbolism connected to this second covenant sacrifice:

- Abraham, at age 115, represented God the Father.
- Isaac, at age 15, was Abraham's only begotten son by promise, and represented Jesus the Messiah—God the Father's only begotten Son.
- Isaac's carrying of the wood for the sacrifice was a type of Christ carrying His crucifixion cross.
- The fact that Isaac was not sacrificed is a demonstration of God's mercy and forgiveness of human sin through the resurrected Christ.
- The ram, as a substitute sacrifice, portrays Jesus' substitute sacrifice as the "Lamb of God Who takes away the sin of the world" for all repentant sinners—i.e., Christ's death instead of theirs.

God made His covenant promises to Abraham irrevocably binding when He proclaimed: "**By Myself have I sworn**." God swore an oath to Abraham *using His own eternal existence* as His personal covenant pledge that He would fulfill His promises. **There can be no greater *guarantee* than God's eternal existence!** Notice also, with this second covenant sacrifice, that God emphasized the spiritual seed *first*: *"I will multiply your seed like the stars of the heavens."* God then unconditionally pledged the coming of the singular Spiritual Seed—Jesus the Christ—by proclaiming that **"in your Seed shall all the nations of the earth be blessed."**[6] This Promised Seed would come through Isaac.[7]

The coming New Covenant through Jesus Christ was made absolutely sure because of Abraham's obedience to God—as He said to him, "because you have obeyed My voice." As we will see later, to "obey the voice of God" involves *much more* than a simple belief in God's existence.

After the death of Abraham, God appeared to his son, Isaac, and told him why the covenant promises were being passed on to him and his future descendants. What God said is very revealing: "And the LORD appeared to him and said, 'Do not go down into Egypt. Live in the land which I shall tell you of. Stay in this land, and I will be with you and bless you, for to you and to your seed, I will give all these lands; and I will establish the oath which I swore to Abraham your father. **And I will multiply your seed as the stars of the heavens** [the spiritual seed] and will give to your seed [the physical seed] all these lands. **And in your seed** [the physical seed *and* the spiritual seed] **shall all the nations of the earth be blessed, because Abraham obeyed My voice and kept My charge, My commandments, My statutes, and My laws'** " (Gen. 26:2-5).

Notice that when God passed the covenant promises on to Isaac, He again emphasized the *spiritual seed*. This "spiritual seed" has everything to do with the *ultimate potential* of man!

In the next chapter we will learn about the actual nature of God, which will be a vital key to answering the question, *Why were you born?*

Chapter 5 Notes:

1. Alexander Hislop, *The Two Babylons*

2. For more on this aspect of God's promises to Abraham, see *America and Britain—Their Biblical Origin and Prophetic Destiny,* Philip Neal, York Publishing, 2014; available at no cost through www.cbcg.org.

3. Other Old Testament prophecies relating to Jesus include:

Gen. 3:15	Dan. 9:26	Psa. 2:7
Deut. 18:15	Isa. 7:14	Psa. 22:1, 16-18

Zech. 9:9	Isa. 52:14	Psa. 34:20
Zech. 12:10	Isa. 53:4-7, 10-12	Psa. 69:21
Zech. 13:7		Psa. 109:25

4. Abraham had been sojourning in the land of Canaan for ten years when he received the promises. Although he believed God, he wanted to know *how* and *when* God would fulfill His promises (Gen 15:8.) God responded by instructing Abraham to prepare a special sacrifice by which He would establish a *unilateral* covenant with Abraham. Specific animals were to be split from head to tail to make a *path* between the halves (Gen. 15:9-10). The participants were required to walk the path between the animal parts.

According to covenantal law, a covenant does not become valid until it has been sealed with a blood sacrifice. The bloody carcasses of the sacrificial animals represented the symbolic death of the one confirming the covenant. By passing between these carcasses, the one who is ratifying the covenant is swearing, by an oath, that if he fails to perform the terms of the covenant *he will die*, and his blood will be spilled on the ground in the same manner as the animals (see Jeremiah 34 as an example of this type of covenant). Once ratified by this maledictory oath, the terms of the covenant cannot be changed—neither by adding to them nor by diminishing from them.

Unlike the example recorded by Jeremiah, the covenant God established with Abraham did not require the patriarch to participate by passing between the pieces of the animals. When we examine the account in Genesis 15, it is clear that *only God* passed between the parts of the animals. In fact, from the late afternoon until dark, Abraham slept through the entire sacrificial ceremony in a symbolic "death sleep" Thus, God was demonstrating that *He alone* was going to *take full responsibility* for the fulfillment of the covenant promises.

5. Abraham was 75 when God called him (Gen. 12:4), and 85 when God made the first covenant sacrifice (Gen. 16:16). The second covenant sacrifice (involving Isaac) came 40 years after Abraham's initial calling. In the Scriptures, the number 40 is indicative of "trial and testing."

6. The apostle Paul writes of Abraham and this promise: "For as many *of you* as were baptized into Christ did put on Christ. There is neither Jew nor Greek; there is neither bond nor free; there is neither male nor female; for you are all one in Christ Jesus. **And if you *are* Christ's, then you are Abraham's seed, and heirs according to *the* promise**" (Gal. 3:27-29).

7. Concerning the spiritual seed, Paul writes, "Now we, brethren, like Isaac, are *the* children of promise" (Gal. 4:28).

The *Family* Nature of God

Central to the purpose of God in creating mankind is the astonishing truth about the *nature* of God—that God is a *Family!* Prior to Jesus' coming, this vital knowledge was "hidden from ages and generations."

While God is eternal and composed of spirit, there is something about the fundamental nature of the Godhead that goes unnoticed by most: **God is plural in nature**—i.e., there is *more than one* Eternal Being in the Godhead. The first allusion to this fact is found in Genesis one. In creating man, God said, "Let **US** make man in **Our** image, after **Our** likeness…" (Gen. 1:26). Notice the plurality—who are the *Us* speaking here?

The Hebrew *Elohim*—A Vital Key

The first clue is found in the word "God." The English word *God* is translated from the Hebrew word *Elohim*, which is a *plural* noun. This word reveals essential knowledge concerning the nature of God. [1] Like English plural nouns, Hebrew plural nouns refer to more than one person or thing. As the plural noun "men" inherently means more than one man, *Elohim* means more than a single God Being. A number of passages in the Old Testament confirm the existence of more than one Divine Being (Gen. 1:26; 11:7; Psa. 110:1; 45:7-8; Dan. 7:13).

In fact, the Scriptures reveal that there are *two* who are *Elohim*. In the Old Testament, one *Elohim* is the God Who is called "the Most High" (Gen. 14:22) and the "Ancient of Days" (Dan. 7:13). In the New Testament He is revealed as "God the Father." The other *Elohim* in the Old Testament is the God Who is called the "LORD God" and the "Almighty God." This is the God Who later *became* Jesus, the Christ of the New Testament.

These fundamental truths are verified by the apostle John, who writes, "In *the* beginning was the Word, and **the Word was with God**, and **the Word was God.** He was in *the* beginning with God. All things came into being through Him, and without Him not even one *thing* came into being. In Him was life, and the life was the light of men…. [And] the **Word was made flesh**, and tabernacled [temporarily dwelt] among us, and we beheld His glory, the glory as of *the* **only begotten with the Father**, full of grace and truth" (John 1:1-4, 14). This substantiates that the "LORD God" of the

Old Testament *became* the "Word" or Jesus Christ of the New Testament, (Matt. 1:21, 25).

The apostle Paul calls Jesus "God manifested in the flesh" (I Tim. 3:16), and notes that He is actually the Creator of all things: "Because by Him [Jesus] were all things created, the things in heaven and the things on earth, the visible and the invisible, whether *they be* thrones, or lordships, or principalities, or powers: **all things were created by Him and for Him**. And He is before all, and by Him all things subsist" (Col. 1:16-17). In fact, Paul uses the entire book of Hebrews to demonstrate that Jesus was indeed the God of the Old Testament and is now the very Son of God: "But we see Jesus, Who *was* made a little lower than *the* angels [made flesh and blood], crowned with glory and honor on account of suffering the death [by crucifixion, for the sin of the world], in order that by *the* grace of God He Himself might taste death for everyone; because it was fitting for Him, **for Whom all things *were created*, and by Whom all things *exist***, in bringing many sons unto glory, to make the Author of their salvation perfect through sufferings" (Heb. 2:9-10).

The New Testament clearly teaches that Jesus was *with* God and *was* God before He became flesh. Thus, Jesus existed from the beginning and was the *Elohim*, or God, of the Old Testament Who became God manifested in the flesh. He was sent to earth by the Father, the other *Elohim* of the Old Testament—"the Most High God" (Psa. 57:2; 78:56).

Indeed, the God Who appeared to all the patriarchs and Who led the children of Israel out of Egypt was the *Elohim* Who became Jesus the Christ (Ex. 3:6-8; I Cor. 10:4). The God Who later became the Father never revealed Himself to man in Old Testament times. In fact, God the Father was not revealed until the coming of Jesus: "**No one has seen God at any time**; the only begotten Son, Who is in the bosom of the Father, **He has declared Him**" (John 1:18). Indeed, a major purpose of Jesus' ministry was to reveal the Father: "**No one knows the Son except the Father; neither does anyone know the Father except the Son, and the one to whom the Son personally chooses to reveal *Him***" (Matt. 11:27).[2]

As we will see in greater detail later, the "Us" of Genesis 1:26 could not be understood until the time of Christ. In His prayer to God the Father, Jesus said, "That they all [the disciples of all time] may be one, even as You, Father, *are* in Me, and I in You; that they also may be one in **US**..." (John 17:21). While most professing Christians believe that there are *three* Persons in the Godhead, there is clear evidence throughout the Bible that there are only *two* Beings who are God (see Appendix 4, *Does the Bible Teach the Trinity?*).

As we will see, this understanding of the nature of God is central to answering the question, *"Why were you born?"* **It is vital to understand that the God of the Old Testament was** *made flesh* **and** *became Jesus,* **the** *Son of God.* This is where the *family aspect* of the Godhead began! At Jesus' birth, one Elohim became the *Father* while the other Elohim became His *Son*—thus, a Divine *Family.* Thus, it is written, "I will declare the decree of the LORD. He has said to Me, '**You are My Son; this day I have begotten You**. Ask of Me, and I shall give the nations for Your inheritance, and the uttermost parts of the earth for Your possession. You shall break them with a rod of iron; You shall dash them in pieces like a potter's vessel' " (Psa. 2:7-9).

As God in the flesh, Jesus was subjected to death—but through a resurrection, He was *made spirit* again, restored to His former eternal glory. As we will see in a later chapter, Jesus was in fact our "forerunner" or "trailblazer," showing the way for man to also enter into that *same* glory!

God Is a Family

The key to understanding the awesome purpose for mankind is to understand first that God is actually a *plurality* of Being's—a Divine Family—presently consisting of the Father and Christ. But God is *expanding* that family—and there will be others who will ultimately bear the family name! (Eph. 3:15).

When God created mankind, He said, " 'Let Us [God the Father and God the Son] make man **in Our image, after Our likeness.**'... And God [Elohim] created man **in His** *own* **image, in the image of God** He created him. He created them male and female" (Gen. 1:26-27). Thus, men and women are created in God's *image* and *likeness,* to be *like Him.*

This language concerns *family.* Indeed, Genesis 5:3 says that Adam "begot a son *in his own likeness, after his image.*" It was after creating plants and animals to reproduce each "according to its kind" that God said, "Let Us make man in Our *image,* after Our *likeness.*" This shows that man was created according to the *God kind.* So God is essentially *reproducing Himself* through humanity!

God has given mankind attributes like His—of the "God kind." David was inspired to write, "O LORD our Lord, how excellent is Your name in all the earth.... When I consider Your heavens, the work of Your fingers, the moon and the stars which You have ordained, [I am compelled to ask,] What is man, that You are mindful of him? ... **You have made him a little lower than God** [*Elohim*]..." (Psa. 8:1-5).

Many translations of the Bible, including the *King James Version*, render this verse as "a little lower than the angels." However, the Hebrew word *Elohim*, as used in this verse, refers to deities—not to angels. This word is used countless times in the Hebrew text in reference to the true God and to false gods. In every other occurrence in the *KJV*, *Elohim* is correctly translated "God" or "gods." In Psalm 8:5, *Elohim* is clearly referring to the true God and should be translated accordingly. Green's translation conveys the correct meaning of the text: "For You have made him lack a little from God." [3]

The correct translation of this verse *reveals the tremendous potential of mankind!* God made man in His image and likeness—but, as we have seen, of an *inferior nature*. We are a "little lower" than God—but only for a time!

Through direct creation, Adam was a *son* of God (Luke 3:38). Therefore, since we are descended from Adam, through procreation we are also the offspring of God. In the New Testament God reveals that on a spiritual level we are His children. He tells us, " 'I will be a Father to you, and *you shall be My sons and daughters,*' says the Lord Almighty" (II Cor. 6:18). Just as both men and women are God's children through *physical creation*, so both can *become* God's children through a *spiritual process* that results in them literally becoming spirit beings—composed of spirit through a special *spiritual creation.*

Although made of flesh, which is subject to sin and corruption, man has the *potential*—according to God's plan—to receive the Holy Spirit of God. And as Jesus tells us we are to become holy and righteous as God is (Matt. 5:48). As we will see in a later chapter, all who attain to the righteousness of God through faith in Jesus the Christ will—by the resurrection from the dead—be *born into the family of God* as immortal spirit beings, composed of the same substance as God.

Indeed, just as all life was made to reproduce after its own kind, God patterned man after the "God kind." It is God's plan and desire to *add to Their kind*—to bring "many sons to glory" (Heb. 2:10). *This is the ultimate purpose for which you were born!*

In the following chapter, we will see that Jesus, the promised Messiah, came as *God in the flesh*. We will learn *how* and *why* the Eternal God—in the person of Jesus—died for man!

Chapter 6 Notes:

1. Additional attributes of the nature of God: God is Spirit (John 4:24). God is eternal, ever-living and self-existent (Deut. 33:27; Isa. 40:28). God is holy (Isa. 57:15). God is love (I John 4:6, 16). God is truth (Deut. 32:4; Psa. 31:5; 33:4; Jer. 4:2; John 14:6). God is Light (I John 1:5). God is Creator (Gen. 1; John 1:1-4). God is Lawgiver and Judge (James 4:12; Isa. 33:22). God is a consuming fire (Heb. 12:29). God is the Savior of all (Psa. 106:21; Isa. 43:3; 45:21-22; 60:16; Hosea 13:4; John 4:42; I Tim. 1:1; 2:3; 4:10; Tit. 1:3-4; 2:10, 13; 3:4, 6; I John 4:14). God is our Redeemer from sin (Psa. 19:14; Isa. 41:14; 49:26; I Pet. 1:18; Rev. 5:9). God is merciful (Psa. 103:8-18; 119:64). God is gracious (Psa. 86:15; 111:4; 112:4; 116:5; I Pet. 2:3; Rom 2:4). God is long-suffering (Rom. 2:4; I Tim. 1:16) and abundant in goodness (Psa. 31:19; 33:5; 107:8, 15, 21, 31). God is forgiving (Psa. 103:1-4; Acts 2:38; 3:19; Rom. 3:23-25).

2. These plain statements show that the God Who manifested Himself to men and women in Old Testament times was not God the Father. John adds to the evidence by recording these words of Jesus: "And the Father Himself, Who sent Me, has borne witness of Me. **You have neither heard His voice nor seen His form at any time**" (John 5:37).

The God Who walked and talked with Adam and Eve was not the Father. The God Who delivered the Ten Commandments to Moses and the children of Israel was not God the Father. The God Who spoke through the prophets was not the Father. No man has ever seen the Father, except Jesus: "And no one has ascended into heaven, except He Who came down from heaven, *even* the Son of man, Who is [now] in heaven [John recorded these words around 90 AD]" (John 3:13).

The Scriptures make it absolutely clear that the Lord God Who appeared to the patriarchs and the prophets of old was Jesus the Christ—not the Father. The words of Jesus Himself reveal that He preexisted as God before He became human. In His prayer to the Father after His last Passover, Jesus said: "I have glorified You on the earth. I have finished the work that You gave Me to do. And now, Father, glorify Me with Your own self, with **the glory that I had with You before the world existed**" (John 17:4-5).

3. J. P. Green, *Interlinear Hebrew-Greek-English Bible*

CHAPTER SEVEN

Jesus Christ and the Redemption
of Man and Woman

According to the Scriptures, God's purpose for the human family included a plan for the *redemption* of mankind. This plan was in place from the foundation of the world, before the creation of Adam and Eve (Rev. 13:8).

But why do human beings need redemption? What do they need to be redeemed from? How is God going to accomplish this redemption? Indeed, what can God *do* to reconcile mankind to Himself?

As we will see, the answer revolves around the all-important role of Jesus the Messiah. Why did Jesus have to come as a man—God manifested in the flesh—and die? How did He and God the Father[1] accomplish such an incredible feat? The answers to these questions are revealed in the Word of God. In order to understand, we must first go back to the creation of man and woman—to consider the magnitude and consequences of their sin.

From the beginning God created within Adam and Eve, and their descendants, the ability to think, reason and plan. He also gave to them independent, free moral agency—the capacity to choose and make decisions. These are all godlike attributes. Although Adam and Eve walked with God daily for a time, they ultimately chose to *decide for themselves* what was good and evil, as depicted by their taking of the "Tree of the Knowledge of Good and Evil."

However, **only God, as Creator and Lawgiver, knows what is truly good and what is truly evil. Man, apart from God and His laws, does *not* have the innate ability to decide what is good or what is evil. That prerogative belongs to God alone!**

Adam and Eve, under the sway of the serpent, Satan the devil, chose to disobey God. The consequences of their sin continues to this day—adversely affecting all of mankind. *Two* **profound consequences resulted**, which only God can resolve through His plan of redemption in Christ.

1) Human nature and death passed to all of the human family. Prior to their sin, Adam and Eve had a nature that was neither for, nor against, God. He had given them *independent free moral agency*—the freedom to make their own choices. He had set before them His way of love and obedience, which would lead to eternal life, as symbolized by the "Tree of Life."

He also set before them the "Tree of the Knowledge of Good and Evil"—representing the choice to reject God and His way. God strictly commanded them to *not* eat of that tree. If they disobeyed and ate of that tree, their sin would result in their death. Thus, they had to choose whether they would love and obey God or not.

Adam and Eve disobeyed God by listening to the serpent and choosing to decide for themselves what was "good" and what was "evil." By so doing, they cut themselves off from God and from access to the Tree of Life. As a result of their sin, by the sentence of God's judgment (Gen. 3:16-19), He permanently *changed their nature* from being neutral toward God to being a mixture of good and evil. Thus, *human nature* became deceitful and hostile toward God and His laws and commandments (Rom. 8:7).

The apostle Paul substantiates this: "Therefore, as by one man sin entered into the world, and by means of sin *came* death; and in this way, **death passed into all mankind;** *and it is* **for this reason that all have sinned**" (Rom. 5:12). And again, "in Adam all die" (I Cor. 15:22). The phrases "death passed into all mankind" and "it is for this reason that all have sinned" verify that man's original neutral nature was *changed* to a nature of sin and death. In fact, Paul specifically calls this subsequent human nature the "law of sin and death" (Rom. 8:2). This is the nature that has been *genetically passed* from Adam and Eve into the hearts and minds of *every generation*.

Consequently, much of the "good" that people do is not of God, but originates with the Tree of the Knowledge of Good and Evil. Such perceived "good" may bring a superficial or temporary "benefit," but it nearly always ends in failure. The Proverbs teach us about deceptive human nature cut off from God and His Word: "There is a way which seems right to a man, but the end thereof *is* the way of death…. All the ways of a man are clean in his own eyes, but the LORD weighs the spirits…. [As a man] thinks in his heart, so *is* he" (Prov. 14:12; 16:2; 23:7).

Human nature is essentially deceitful, evil, and self-destructive. Even God lamented over the pervasive, universal evil of Noah's generation before the Flood: "And the LORD saw that **the wickedness of man** *was* **great on the earth, and every imagination of the thoughts of his heart** *was* **only evil continually**…. Now the earth also was corrupt before God, and the earth was filled with violence. And God looked upon the earth, and behold, it was corrupt—for **all flesh had corrupted its way upon the earth**" (Gen. 6:4, 11-12).

Over 1,800 years later, the prophet Jeremiah declared that human nature was still the same: "**The heart** *is* **deceitful above all things, and desperately wicked; who can know it?**… O LORD, I know that the way of man is not in himself; *it is* not in man who walks to direct his steps" (Jer. 17:9; 10:23).

Hundreds of years after Jeremiah, Jesus said that from the depths of human nature comes sin, evil and wickedness: "That which springs forth from *within* a man, that defiles the man. **For from within, out of the hearts of men**, go forth evil thoughts, adulteries, fornications, murders, thefts, covetousness, wickednesses, guile, licentiousness, an evil eye, blasphemy, pride *and* foolishness. **All these evils go forth from within**, and *these* defile a man" (Mark 7:20-23).[2]

These passages verify that human nature—the "law of sin and death"— can never be changed or overcome *apart from God.*

2) Mankind is held captive to Satan's deceptive rule. Adam and Eve listened to Satan instead of God. Because of their sin, Satan became the "god of this world"—i.e., this *present age* (II Cor. 4:4). From that time forward, all of mankind has been under the sway and deception of Satan (Rev. 12:9)—except for those few God has chosen to call in this age. While tempting Jesus to worship him, Satan bragged, "I will give You all this authority [over all the nations], and the glory of them *all*; for it has been delivered [during this age] to me, and I give it to whomever I desire" (Luke 4:6). Indeed, unto this day "the whole world lies in *the power of* the wicked one" (I John 5:19). Moreover, in the end time in which we are now living, it has been prophesied that the whole world will worship Satan and the Antichrist (Rev. 13:3-4).

Thus, as a result of God's judgment for their sin, these two major consequences came upon Adam and Eve and their descendants. Despite all of mankind's "good" intentions, over 6,000 years of history has proven that without God it is impossible for mankind—enslaved to sin and death—to solve the lawlessness of human nature. Man simply does not have the ability to overcome Satan. Paul writes: "Because the creation was subjected to vanity, not willingly, but by reason of Him who subjected *it* in hope, in order that the creation itself might be delivered from the bondage of corruption [sin and death and Satan] into the freedom of the glory of the children of God. For we know that all the creation is groaning together and travailing together until now" (Rom. 8:20-22).

As we will see, because of God's great love for mankind, He has purposed to redeem the human family from sin, death and Satan—through His Son, Jesus the Christ.

God Becomes a Man

In the greatest manifestation of the love of God, the Creator of mankind, in the most astounding act of humility, *became a man*. There are two little-known reasons why God created man in *His image* and after *His likeness*. The first reason was so that *God could become a man* to redeem mankind from sin. The second reason is so that *those who are redeemed could become like God* (which will be addressed later).

The Lord God Who had created man from the dust of the ground came to the earth in the flesh as Jesus Christ, as John writes: "In *the* beginning was the Word, and the Word was with God, and the Word was God. He was in *the* beginning with God. All things came into being through Him, and not even one *thing* that was created came into being without Him…. And the Word became flesh, and tabernacled [temporarily dwelt] among us (and we ourselves beheld His glory, *the* glory as of *the* only begotten with *the* Father), full of grace and truth" (John 1:1-3, 14).

Paul gives additional details as to *how* God was able to become a man: "Let this mind be in you, which *was* also in Christ Jesus, Who, although He existed [Greek *huparchoon*, to exist or preexist] **in the form of God**, did not consider it robbery to be equal with God, but **emptied Himself** [of His power and glory], *and* was made in the likeness [Greek *homoioma*, the same existence] of men *and* took the form of a servant [Greek *doulos*, a slave], and being found in *the* manner of man, **He humbled Himself, and became obedient unto death**, even the death of the cross" (Phil. 2:5-8).

These inspired words of Paul confirm that before Jesus became human, He was, in fact, one of *Elohim*, the Lord God of the Old Testament. Existing as God, He was composed of ever-living Spirit; and as God, composed of spirit, it was impossible for Him to die.

Think on this: The God Who created man in His image and likeness took on the same substance as man. Paul reveals that the one of *Elohim* Who became Christ "emptied Himself" of His glory and power as God in order to be made in the likeness of man. The great and glorious God, Creator of the heavens and earth and all that is in them, *relinquished being God* in the greatest, most awesome act of love and humility—in order to redeem and save mankind!

In emptying Himself of His glory as God, He placed Himself under the power of God the Father, Who reduced Him to only a pinpoint of life. Then God the Father, by the power of His Holy Spirit, joined this pinpoint of life to an ovum within the virgin Mary's womb. Thus, Jesus became the "only begotten" Son of God.

But *why* was it obligatory for God to become *flesh*—a man? What kind of flesh did God take upon Himself when He became Jesus Christ? Was His flesh the same as all human flesh? As we will see, in order for God to redeem man from the "law of sin and death" and Satan the devil, it was *necessary for Him to die*. Consequently, the only way for God to die was to become human—to be "manifested in the flesh." Astonishingly, He did not suddenly appear as a fully mature man. Rather, He was reduced to a *pinpoint of life* in order to become a man—beginning with conception, as are all other men and women.

When Mary asked the angel Gabriel how it was possible for her to conceive, not having had sexual relations with a man, he answered, "*The* Holy Spirit shall come upon you, and **the power of *the* Highest** shall overshadow you; wherefore **the Holy One *which is* being begotten** [the Greek means that the impregnation was taking place at that very moment] *in you* **shall also be called *the* Son of God**" (Luke 1:35).

At the instant Jesus was conceived in the womb of Mary, He became the only divinely begotten Son of God the Father, fulfilling the prophecy of Psalm 2: "He [the *Elohim* Who became the Father] said, '**You *are* My Son; this day have I begotten You**' " (verse 7).

In addition, Jesus revealed that He had authority from the Father to lay down His life and to receive it back again. Notice: "On account of this, the Father loves Me, because I lay down My life, that I may receive it back again. No one takes it from Me, but I lay it down of Myself. **I have authority to lay it down and authority to receive it back again. This commandment I received from My Father**" (John 10:17-18). As Paul shows, Jesus gave His body as the one perfect sacrifice for sin—once for all time (Heb. 10:10).

Jesus said of Himself: "I am the living bread, which came down from heaven. If anyone eats of this bread, he shall live forever; and **the bread that I will give is My flesh, which I will give for the life of the world**" (John 6:51). In order to give His flesh for the life of the world, Christ had to be fully human. He had to share and experience the full range of human existence, with human nature—from conception and birth to childhood, adulthood and death.

Jesus Christ Shared the Human Experience

In writing to the Hebrews, Paul used many passages from the Old Testament to show that Jesus shared the same mortal existence as all human beings. His inspired explanation of Psalm 8 makes this clear. The suffering and death of Christ were essential to the fulfillment of God's purpose for man: "But in a certain place one fully testified, saying, 'What is man, that

You [Yourself] are mindful of him, or *the* son of man, that You [Yourself] visit him? You did make him a little lower than *the* angels; You did crown him with glory and honor, and *You* did set him over the works of Your hands; You did put all things in subjection under his feet.' For in subjecting all things to him, He left nothing *that was* not subjected to him. But now we do not yet see all things subjected to him [man].

"But we see Jesus, Who *was* made a little lower than *the* angels, crowned with glory and honor on account of suffering the death, in order that **by the grace of God He Himself might taste [partake of] death for everyone**; because it was fitting for Him, for Whom *are* all things, and by Whom *are* all things, in bringing many sons unto glory, to make the Author of their salvation perfect through sufferings" (Heb. 2:6-10).

What a magnificent expression of God's love! The Creator of all mankind temporarily gave up His eternal existence as God and lowered Himself to the level of mortal man, so that He could suffer and die for every human being. Think of it! By the grace and love of God, through the power of the Holy Spirit, He willingly took upon Himself the death penalty that had come upon all mankind through sin. Because He is the Creator of all mankind, the death of Christ through His shed blood is the only sacrifice that can bring forgiveness of human sin: "Therefore, since the children have partaken of flesh and blood, **in like manner He also took part in the same** [flesh and blood], in order that through [His] death He might annul him who has the power of death—that is, the devil.

"And *that* He might deliver those who were subject to bondage all through their lives by *their* fear of death. For surely, He is not taking upon Himself to help the angels; but He is taking upon Himself to help the seed [the promised spiritual seed] of Abraham. **For this reason, it was obligatory for *Him* to be made like His brethren in everything** [sharing the same flesh and nature], that He might be a merciful and faithful High Priest *in* things pertaining to God, in order to make propitiation [to bring forgiveness] for the sins of the people. Because He Himself has suffered, having been tempted *in like manner*, He is able to help those who are being tempted" (Heb. 2:14-18). Paul leaves no room for doubt that Jesus was fully human.

In Genesis 15, the one of *Elohim* Who later became Jesus entered into a covenant with Abraham by taking a maledictory oath. He thus obligated Himself to die in order to fulfill the promises of the covenant for the spiritual seed. [3] The covenant required His death. In other words, the Lord God obligated Himself to become flesh and blood—a mortal subject to death (Heb. 10:5-10). This was His covenant pledge.

But the promises could not be fulfilled by His death alone. In order to fulfill the promise of spiritual seed by redeeming mankind, it was necessary for Jesus to be resurrected from the dead and become mankind's personal Mediator and High Priest in heaven. For this reason, He took on the *same nature* that all humans share. Because He experienced the same temptations, yet without sin, Jesus is uniquely able to make intercession before the Father for anyone who repents of their sins. Moreover, He is able to provide the spiritual strength to overcome the pulls of human nature and the influence of Satan.

Jesus Took the "Law of Sin and Death" Within Himself

The Bible teaches that Jesus Christ was fully human, sharing the same flesh that all mankind has—*including* the "law of sin and death." It is important to understand this truth. Paul specifically describes the flesh of Jesus in this manner: "For what was impossible for the law *to do*, in that it was weak through the flesh [because of the *law of sin and death* within human flesh], God, having sent His own Son **in *the* likeness of sinful flesh, and for sin, condemned sin in the flesh** [Jesus' flesh]" (Rom. 8:3). A literal translation of the Greek is "**in *the* likeness of flesh, of sin**...." The word "likeness" is translated from the Greek *homoioomati*, which means "likeness, the same" (Arndt and Gingrich, *A Greek-English Lexicon of the New Testament*).

That Jesus was made in the "likeness of sinful flesh" leaves no doubt that the "law of sin and death" was passed on to Jesus from His mother Mary. Because Jesus had to be fully human, He had to inherit the "law of sin and death." If He did not have the "law of sin and death" within His fleshly body, He would not have been fully human! This means He had the *potential* to sin at any time during His human life. If, as some claim, Jesus was incapable of sin, it would have been impossible for Him to be tempted. Thus, the devil could not have tempted Jesus in the wilderness, as the Scriptures record (Matt. 4:1-11; Mark 1:12-13; Luke 4:1-13).

The fact that Jesus experienced this temptation by Satan shows that the "law of sin and death" was within His flesh. On the other hand, through the power of the Holy Spirit, He was able to resist the desires and pulls of the flesh through which Satan was tempting Him to sin. Thus, Jesus never sinned, as He knew that those who succumb to the lusts of the flesh are practicing the ways of Satan.

During His ministry, Jesus openly condemned the Jewish religious leaders for following Satan. He said, "You are of *your* father the devil, and the lusts of your father you desire to practice. He was a murderer from *the* beginning, and has not stood in the truth, because there is no truth in him. Whenever he speaks a lie, he is speaking from his own *self*; for he is a liar, and the father of it" (John 8:44). Jesus then made a statement showing that He had the potential to sin: "And you have not known Him [God the Father]; but I know Him. And **if I should say that I do not know Him, I shall be, like you, a liar**" (John 8:55). Thus, it was *possible* for Jesus to lie if He had *chosen* to do so. But, unlike the Jewish religious leaders, Jesus always chose to do the things that pleased the Father (John 8:29).

Since Jesus had the same flesh and the same nature as all human beings, *He was tempted*. Because He was tempted, He was capable of sinning—if He chose to sin. However, if Jesus *had* sinned, He would have incurred the penalty of death for Himself, because He was made subject to the Law. Paul writes: "But when the time for the fulfillment came [the time in God's plan to fulfill the prophecy of the Messiah], God sent forth His own Son, born of a woman, **born under Law, in order that He might redeem those who are under Law**, so that we might receive the *gift of* sonship *from God*" (Gal. 4:4-5).

In Romans 7:5 through 8:2, Paul describes in detail how the "law of sin and death" works in every human being to bring forth death. Jesus overcame every temptation, *and* the "law of sin and death," through the power of the Holy Spirit. This is why only His sacrifice and His shed blood can deliver human beings from their sinful nature that leads to eternal death.

During His 40 days of temptation by Satan, Jesus chose to humble Himself by fasting rather than nourish His flesh. He relied on the Word of God and the power of the Holy Spirit from God the Father. He did not trust in His own strength and His own mind.

If Jesus had no potential to sin, there would have been absolutely no reason for Him to undergo such a brutal temptation. In other words, if it had been impossible for Jesus to sin, His temptation by Satan would have served no purpose. Without the *potential* for sin and the *possibility* of being influenced by the pulls of the flesh, there would have been no way for Jesus to actually experience temptation as all humans have (James 1:14-15).

In his epistle to the Hebrews, Paul writes of the great struggle that Jesus experienced to never yield to a single temptation and to never sin. He writes: "[Jesus,] Who, in the days of His flesh, offered up both prayers and supplications with strong crying and tears to Him Who was able to save Him from death, and was heard because *He* feared *God*. Although He was a Son, *yet* He learned obedience from the things that He suffered; and having been perfected [through His life as a human being], He became *the* Author of eternal salvation to all those who obey Him" (Heb. 5:7-9).

In order for Jesus to qualify as our "Author of salvation," He had to experience the same temptations that beset all humans: "For we do not have a High Priest who cannot empathize with our weaknesses, but *one Who was*

tempted in all things [in every way] **according to** *the* **likeness of** *our temptations*; **yet** *He was* **without sin**. Because of this, we ourselves should come with boldness to the throne of grace, so that we may receive mercy and find grace to help in time of need" (Heb. 4:15-16).

The phrase "according to *the* likeness of" is translated from the Greek *kath omoioteeta*, which literally means "in every way just as we are." In other words, while Jesus was in the flesh, He experienced exactly the same temptations that we do because He was made in the "likeness of sinful flesh." Yet Jesus never sinned because He never yielded to a single temptation of the flesh or of Satan the devil.

According to Paul, this is how God condemned sin in the flesh—the flesh of Christ: "For what *was* impossible for the law to do, in that it was weak through the flesh, God, having sent His own Son in *the* likeness of sinful flesh, and for sin, **condemned sin in the flesh**" (Rom. 8:3).

In order for God to carry out His awesome plan and purpose for mankind, He fulfilled His covenant pledge to provide redemption and to conquer Satan. He did so by becoming a man with all the attributes of human nature. He overcame Satan the devil and condemned sin in His own literal flesh. Because Jesus never sinned, God the Father accepted His death as the only *full payment* for all human sin, as the wages of sin is death. As we will see in Chapter 8, this opened the next phase of God's plan—the redemption and salvation of the *spiritual seed* from all nations.

Chapter 7 Notes:

1. The two *Elohim* of the Old Testament are the "Most High God," Who became the Father, *and* the "LORD God," who became the Son, Jesus Christ.

2. Paul also writes of the unregenerate evil of mankind, which typifies *all* of human civilization: "**For we have already charged both Jews and Gentiles—ALL—*with* being under sin**, exactly as it is written: 'For there is not a righteous one—not even one! There is not one who understands; there is not one who seeks after God. They have all gone out of the way; together they have *all* become depraved. There is not *even* one who is practicing kindness. No, there is not so much as one! Their throats *are* like an open grave; with their tongues they have used deceit; *the* venom of asps *is* under their lips, whose mouths are full of cursing and bitterness; their feet *are* swift to shed blood; destruction and misery *are* in their ways; and *the* way of peace they have not known. There is no fear of God before their eyes.' Now then, **we know that whatever the law says, it speaks to those who are under the law, so that every mouth may be stopped, and all the world may become guilty before God**" (Rom. 3:9-19).

Paul also describes "works of the flesh": "Now the works of the flesh are manifest, which are *these*: adultery, fornication, uncleanness, licentiousness, idolatry, witchcraft, hatred, strifes, jealousies, indignations, contentions, divisions, sects, envyings, murders, drunkenness, revelings, and such things as these" (Gal. 5:19-21).

3. God's plan for Abraham's *physical seed* is being fulfilled through the physical tribes of Israel. For a detailed look at this national aspect of the Abrahamic covenant, please request the book *America and Britain—Their Biblical Origin and Prophetic Destiny.*

CHAPTER EIGHT

What Jesus Christ Teaches
About Eternal Life

In the Old Testament, salvation and eternal life was given to only a select few—namely the patriarchs, some kings of Judah, and the prophets. God's covenant with the twelve tribes of Israel, the *physical* seed of Abraham, did not contain promises of spiritual salvation and eternal life. Rather, God's promises and blessings to them were limited to the physical or material realm (Deut. 28; Lev. 26). Nevertheless, the Old Testament does contain a few prophecies concerning the resurrection and eternal life.

It was through Jesus that God first began to reveal the promises of the Holy Spirit and eternal life to the apostles and disciples of Christ. The Gospels of Matthew, Mark, Luke and John contain narratives of Jesus' life, ministry, death by crucifixion, and resurrection. These accounts are not mere traditions that were orally transmitted for hundreds of years before being written down. Rather, as Luke records, written records of Jesus' teachings were made by His disciples throughout His ministry—including accounts of His healings and miracles: "Since many have taken in hand to compile a *written* narration of the matters which have been fully believed [and accomplished] among us, as they delivered *them* to us, **those who from *the* beginning had been eyewitnesses and ministers of the Word** [those who recorded the teachings and events], it seemed good to me also, having accurately understood everything from the very first, to write *these things* in an orderly sequence to you, most excellent Theophilus, so that you might know the *absolute* certainty of *the* things in which you have been instructed" (Luke 1:1-4).

In this chapter, we will focus on Jesus' teachings about salvation and how a person may receive eternal life.[1]

The most frequently quoted verse in the Bible gives us an overview of God's "master plan" for mankind: "For God so loved the world that He gave His only begotten Son, so that everyone who believes in Him may not perish, but may have everlasting life" (John 3:16). This simple, yet profound passage introduces a number of little-understood aspects of God's plan, some of which are yet future. In fact, this verse reaches back in time to God's creation of Adam and Eve *and* projects forward to the New Heavens and the New Earth.

God the Father's *love* is so awesome and all-encompassing that the vast majority of mankind will be given an opportunity to receive eternal life. This is why Jesus said, " 'I am the Alpha and the Omega, *the* Beginning and *the* Ending,' says the Lord, 'Who is, and Who was, and Who *is* to come—the Almighty' " (Rev. 1:8; 22:13; Isa. 46:10). (Today is not the only time for salvation, as God will ultimately make salvation available to every person who desires it. See Appendix 3 for an overview of this vital truth.)

Mark writes that when Jesus began His ministry in Galilee He proclaimed repentance of sin and the Kingdom of God. "The beginning of the gospel of Jesus Christ, *the* Son of God.... Jesus came into Galilee, proclaiming the gospel of the kingdom of God, and saying, 'The time has been fulfilled [for Him to begin His ministry], and the kingdom of God is near at hand [because He personally represented that kingdom]; repent [of sin], and believe in the gospel [the entire message and all the teachings of Christ]' " (Mark 1:14-15).

When the above passages are combined with John 3:16, we see the *steps* a person must take in order to receive eternal life.

First: We have to believe in Jesus Christ. This means that we *know* and *believe* that Jesus is the *only* begotten Son of God the Father—and that He is the Savior of the world, as well as our *personal* Savior. He alone is the Creator of the heavens and earth—and everything in them. He is the personal Creator of all human beings. This is why we *must* believe in Him. Notice what Jesus told the religious Jews who did not believe in Him: "And He said to them, 'You are from beneath; I am from above. You are of this world; I am not of this world. That is why I said to you that you shall die in your sins; **for if you do not believe that I AM, you shall die in your sins**' " (John 8:23-24). When Jesus told them that He was, in fact, the "I AM"—the God of the Old Testament manifested in the flesh—they were greatly afraid. Yet they *still* did not believe in Him.

Second: We are also to believe the Gospel—that is, *every word* of Jesus' message (I Tim. 6:3). We cannot pick and choose which parts of the Gospel message we like and reject the rest. Unfortunately, this is exactly what most mainstream "Christian" ministers do. Even the Catholic Pope at Rome claims he has the power to change the Ten Commandments!

When some of Jesus' disciples were offended at what He taught, they left Him and the other disciples. "These things He said in *the* synagogue as He was teaching in Capernaum. Therefore, after hearing *these words*, many of His disciples said, 'This is a hard saying. Who is able to hear *it*?' But Jesus, knowing that His disciples were complaining about this, said to them, 'Does this offend you? What if you shall see the Son of man ascending up *to* where He was before?

" 'It is the Spirit that gives life; the flesh profits nothing. <u>The words that I speak to you, *they* are spirit and *they* are life</u>. But there are some of you who do not believe.' For Jesus knew from *the* beginning who were the ones that did not believe, and who would betray Him. And He said, 'For this reason, I have said to you, no one can come to Me unless it has been given to him from My Father.'

"From that *time*, many of His disciples went back and walked no more with Him. Therefore, Jesus said to the twelve, 'Are you also desiring to go away?' Then Simon Peter answered Him, '**Lord, to whom shall we go? <u>You have the words of eternal life</u>**; and we have believed and have known that You are the Christ, the Son of the living God' " (John 6:59-69).

Third: We have to repent of our sins, which are the transgressions of the laws and commandments of God (I John 3:4, *KJV*). Repentance means we are greatly sorrowful for our sins against God. We are to *turn away* from living a sinful life and *turn to God* with all of our being: " 'Therefore even now,' says the LORD, 'turn to Me with all your heart, and with fasting, and with weeping, and with mourning. Yes, rend your heart and not your garments, and return to the LORD your God: for He *is* gracious and merciful, slow to anger, and of great kindness…' " (Joel 2:12-13).

Then we are to live the way of God through Jesus Christ. We need to realize that Jesus gave Himself as the ultimate sacrifice for all human sin. His death is the only acceptable payment for our sins (John 1:29, 36). This means we *all* had a part in killing Him! This is why we are to be deeply sorrowful for our sins. Jesus also teaches that unless we repent of our sins, we will *perish*—we will not be saved or receive eternal life. He said: "Now at the same time, *there* were present some who were telling Him about the Galileans, whose blood Pilate had mingled with their sacrifices. And Jesus answered *and* said to them, 'Do you suppose that these Galileans were sinners above all Galileans, because they suffered such things? No, I tell you; but **if you do not repent, you shall all likewise perish**. Or those eighteen on whom the tower in Siloam fell, and killed them, do you suppose that these were debtors above all men who dwelt in Jerusalem? No, I tell you; but **if you do not repent, you shall all likewise perish**' " (Luke 13:1-5).

This is the very reason Jesus had to die and be resurrected from the dead. After He was resurrected and appeared to His disciples, Jesus commissioned them to preach repentance and forgiveness of sins: "And [Jesus] said to them, 'According as it is written, it was necessary for the Christ to suffer, and to rise from *the* dead the third day. And in His name, **repentance and remission of sins should be preached to all nations**, beginning at Jerusalem' " (Luke 24:46-47).

Fourth: To receive eternal life, Jesus taught that we must *keep the commandments* of God. "Now at that time, one came to Him *and* said, 'Good Master, what good *thing* shall I do, that I may have eternal life?' And He said to him, 'Why do you call Me good? No one *is* good except one—God. But **if you desire to enter into life, keep the commandments**' " (Matt. 19:16-17). The young man who had approached Jesus was already keeping many of the commandments of God—according to the *letter* of the law. But Jesus told him that if he wanted to receive eternal life he should sell everything he had. When the young man heard that, he walked away and declined to follow Jesus. He apparently thought more of his wealth than eternal life (verses 18-22).

The young man's wealth had become an *idol*—thus, he was breaking the very first and second commandments. Today, many people keep *some* of the commandments, but they especially stop short of keeping the Sabbath command. And like the young man in Matthew 19, nearly everyone has some kind of *idolatry* in their life.

Likewise, *many* have heard the name of Jesus Christ, yet *very few* are willing to repent, believe, and obey Him—to love God and keep His commandments! All professing Christians have Bibles, but they ignore certain key scriptures—like this one: "By this *standard* we know that we love the children of God: when **we love God and keep His commandments. For this is the love of God: that we keep His commandments; and His commandments are not burdensome**" (I John 5:2-3).

Admittedly, some Bible passages are hard to understand, but this one is *absolutely clear*. Here are two more: Jesus said, "**If you love Me, keep the commandments—namely, My commandments…. If you keep My commandments, you shall live in My love**; just as I have kept My Father's commandments and live in His love" (John 14:15; 15:10).

How Are We to Love God? Since Jesus willingly gave His life for us so that we might have our sins forgiven and receive eternal life, we must *lose our lives in Christ*. What does that mean? Jesus explains, "The one who loves his life shall lose it, and **the one who hates his life in this world shall keep it unto eternal life. If anyone will serve Me, let him follow Me**; and where I am, there shall My servant be also. And if anyone serves Me, him shall the Father honor" (John 12:25-26).

To "hate our lives" means we are not to let anything or anyone *except God* be first in our lives—in our minds and hearts. Jesus further explains, "And great multitudes were going with Him; and He turned *and* said to them, '**If anyone comes to Me and does not hate his father, and mother, and wife, and children, and brothers and sisters, and, in addition, his own life also, he cannot be My disciple**. And whoever does not carry his cross and come after Me [that is, follow in His footsteps] cannot be My disciple" (Luke 14:25-27).

Please understand that we are *not* to actually hate anyone! What Jesus means is that we are to love others *less*, by comparison, than we love God. In putting God first, we love others less—but we do love them. In Matthew 10, Jesus shows that we are to put *following Him* above all else: "**The one who loves father or mother more than Me is not worthy of Me; and the one who loves son or daughter more than Me is not worthy of Me**. And the one who does not take up his cross and follow Me is not worthy of Me" (verses 37-38).

To *love* God the Father and Jesus Christ is so much more than an emotional expression. Rather, such love demands complete devotion to God—with one's entire being! Jesus tells us how we are to love God: "And one of them, a doctor of the law, questioned *Him*, tempting Him, and saying, 'Master, which commandment *is the* great commandment in the Law?' And Jesus said to him, 'You shall love *the* Lord your God with all your heart, and with all your soul, and with all your mind.' **This is *the* first and greatest commandment**. And *the* second *one is* like it: 'You shall love your neighbor as yourself.' **On these two commandments hang all the Law and the Prophets**' " (Matt. 22:35-40). This is why the Law and the Prophets were never abolished, because they fully reflect godly love!

These first four points are the beginning requirements for receiving eternal life. However, in order actually receive eternal life, God has one more essential requirement.

Fifth: We must be baptized by full immersion in water and receive the gift of the Holy Spirit from God the Father. Just before Jesus ascended into heaven, He instructed His apostles and disciples to go into all the world, make disciples, baptize them, and teach them to observe everything He had commanded. "And Jesus came *and* spoke to them, saying, 'All authority in heaven and on earth has been given to Me. Therefore, go *and* make disciples in all nations, baptizing them into the name of the Father, and of the Son, and of the Holy Spirit; teaching them to observe all things that I have commanded you. And lo, I am with you always, *even* until the completion of the age.' Amen" (Matt. 28:18-20).

In the parallel account in Mark, Jesus makes it clear that *baptism* is necessary for salvation. "And He said to them, 'Go into all the world and preach the gospel to the whole creation. **The one who believes and is baptized shall be saved** [receive the gift of eternal life], but the one who does not believe shall be condemned" (Mark 16:15-16).

After Jesus was with the disciples for 40 days following His resurrection, He commanded them to remain in Jerusalem until they received the power of the Holy Spirit. On the Day of Pentecost, when the apostles and disciples were gathered together at the Temple in Jerusalem, God sent the Holy Spirit in a great display of power. God performed a great miracle on that day. When the apostles began preaching the Gospel to the multitudes gathered there, they spoke in a variety of languages. They proved that Jesus' birth, life, death and resurrection fulfilled many Old Testament prophecies.

Then Peter called on the people to repent of their sins—for having a part in crucifying Jesus. He instructed them to be *baptized* in His name: " 'Therefore, let all *the* house of Israel know with full assurance that God has made this *same* Jesus, Whom you crucified, both Lord and Christ.' Now after hearing *this*, they were cut to the heart; and they said to Peter and the other apostles, 'Men *and* brethren, what shall we do?'

"Then Peter said to them, '**Repent and be baptized each one of you in the name of Jesus Christ for *the* remission of sins, and you yourselves shall receive the gift of the Holy Spirit**. For the promise is to you and to your children, and to all those who are afar off, **as many as *the* Lord our God may call**.'

"And with many other words he earnestly testified and exhorted, saying, 'Be saved from this perverse generation.' Then those who joyfully received his message were baptized; and about three thousand souls were added that day" (Acts 2:36-41).

In the next chapter we will see why Jesus said, "Many are called, but few are chosen." As we will see, this is one of the great mysteries of God's marvelous plan!

Chapter 8 Note:

1. It is beyond the scope of this book to delve into all four of the Gospel accounts of Jesus' life, from His birth to His death and resurrection. However, in *A Harmony of the Gospels—the Life of Jesus Christ*, the author presents a complete, detailed account of Jesus' life as God manifested in the flesh. Chronologies and commentaries are included. Please see the "Other Works" page for ordering information.

Why Are Many Called, But Few Chosen?

The Orthodox Christian world teaches that from the time of Jesus' ministry God has been trying to "save" mankind. But when we observe world conditions today—and consider that Christianity itself is rapidly declining—we can only conclude that God is *failing* in His efforts to "save" the world. Is this really the case? Is God *now* trying to "save the world"? As we will see, from the time of Jesus' ministry to His soon-coming return (about 2,000 years), **"many are called but few are chosen"** to receive eternal life (Matt. 20:16; 22:14).

Why is that? First, we need to consider the state of modern Christianity. We know there are billions of Bibles in the world, in many languages.[1] The Bible is also available to hundreds of millions of people through digital devices, with the numbers soaring into the billions. Even though the Word of God is readily available, and professing "Christians" supposedly believe in the name of Christ, they know little to nothing about what the Bible actually teaches—let alone grasp God's true plan of salvation.

How can that be? If we look around the world, we can see that men have formed innumerable "Christian" denominations with billions of followers. Yet, as unfathomable as it may seem, these churches are *not* of God. Rather, they are *counterfeit versions* of Christianity.[2] Such spurious organizations use certain parts of the Bible to present a veneer of Christianity. But what they teach has little relevance to the original Christianity Jesus taught. For example, few ministers teach their followers to truly repent of their sins—and claim that the Law has been abolished. Instead of clear biblical directives, they believe and follow the *traditions* of their religious affiliations. This is why most people are unwilling to believe the Bible, obey God, and keep His commandments!

Jesus revealed to His disciples that *many* people would, over time, hear the call of God, but only a *few* would actually respond to that call. The fact is, only those who truly believe in Jesus, repent of their sins, are baptized, and receive the Holy Spirit are *chosen* to receive eternal life. They are the ones who sincerely love God and keep His commandments in spirit and truth—and will always remain *faithful* (Rev. 17:14).

As Jesus warned His disciples, the majority of people would follow the broad, easy way of human nature—the way that leads to destruction. They tend to follow false teachers and false prophets who *claim* to represent Jesus.[3] Indeed, this has been true of every generation since Jesus' time. Notice His warning:

"**Enter in through the narrow gate; for wide *is* the gate and broad *is* the way that leads to destruction, and many are those who enter through it** [Is this not where the world is headed today?]; <u>**for narrow *is* the gate and difficult *is* the way that leads to life, and few are those who find it**</u>.

"**But beware of false prophets who come to you in sheep's clothing, for within *they* are ravening wolves**. You shall know them by their fruits. They do not gather grapes from thorns, or figs from thistles, do they? In the same way, every good tree produces good fruit, but a corrupt tree produces evil fruit. A good tree cannot produce evil fruit, nor can a corrupt tree produce good fruit. Every tree *that is* not producing good fruit is cut down and is cast into the fire. Therefore, you shall assuredly know them by their fruits.

"**Not everyone who says to Me, 'Lord, Lord,' shall enter into the kingdom of heaven; but the one who is doing** [practicing and obeying] **the will of My Father,** Who *is* in heaven.

"Many [all of the ministers of today's false Christianity] will say to Me in that day [the day of judgment], 'Lord, Lord, did we not prophesy through Your name? And *did we not* cast out demons through Your name? And *did we not* perform many works of power through Your name?' And then I will confess to them, 'I never knew you. **Depart from Me, you who work lawlessness** [and teach that the Law has been abolished, when Jesus said He did not come to abolish the Law or the Prophets (Matt. 5:17-18)].'

"Therefore, **everyone** [the few] **who hears these words of Mine and practices them** [as a way of life], I will compare him to a wise man, who built his house upon the rock; and the rain came down, and the floods came, and the winds blew, and beat upon that house; but it did not fall, for it was founded upon the rock [that Rock is Jesus Christ (I Cor. 10:4)].

"And everyone [the majority] who hears these words of Mine and does not practice them shall be compared to a foolish man, who built his house upon the sand; and the rain came down, and the floods came, and the winds blew, and beat upon that house; and it fell, and great was the fall of it" (Matt. 7:13-27).

Lack of True Belief and Obedience Brings Automatic Spiritual Blindness: As He began His ministry, Jesus personally called and chose the twelve original apostles.[4] He trained them for three and a half years—progressively teaching them much spiritual truth.

On the other hand, in His public messages to the multitudes that followed Him, Jesus often spoke in *parables*. Realizing that parables typically *cloud the truth*, Jesus' disciples asked: " 'Why do You speak to them in parables?' And He answered *and* said to them, '**Because it has been given to you** [the few] **to know the mysteries of the kingdom of heaven, but to them** [the multitudes] **it has not been given**. For whoever has *understanding* [the few who have been chosen], to him more shall be given, and he shall have an abundance; but whoever does not have *understanding* [the many, those not chosen], even what he has shall be taken away from him.

" 'For this *reason* I speak to them in parables, because seeing, they see not; and hearing, they hear not; neither do they understand. And in them is fulfilled the prophecy of Isaiah, which says, "**In hearing you shall hear, and in no way understand; and *in* seeing you shall see, and in no way perceive; for the heart of this people has grown fat, and their ears are dull of hearing, and their eyes they have closed...**" ' " (Matt. 13:10-15).

Multitudes of people followed Jesus, heard Him speak, and saw His miracles and healings. Yes, they desired to see Him, to hear Him, and to be healed by Him; but they refused to believe and obey Him. In so doing, they brought upon themselves automatic spiritual blindness.

After quoting Isaiah, Jesus made an incredible statement. He declared that because the multitudes refused to believe, He *did not want* them to understand and be converted at that time! Though they heard the *call*, their refusal to repent, believe and obey meant that they could not be *chosen* at that time. This is why Jesus spoke to them in parables. This verifies what He said, that "many are called, but only a few are chosen"—because only the *few* truly believe God and repent. Notice how Jesus described the spiritual condition of the multitudes: They were *dull of hearing* and had *closed their eyes*—"**lest they should see with their eyes, and should hear with their ears, and should understand with their hearts, and should be converted, and I should heal them**" (Matt. 13:15).

Overwhelmingly, most people have continued in this way since Jesus' time. Because they refuse to believe, they inflict spiritual blindness upon themselves. Again, this is why "many are called, but few are chosen."

On the other hand, notice what Jesus said to His *few* chosen disciples who had answered His call: "**But blessed *are* your eyes, because they see; and your ears, because they hear**.... Therefore, hear the parable of the sower: When anyone hears the Word of the kingdom and does not understand *it*, the wicked one comes and snatches away that which was sown in his heart. This is the one who was sown by the way. Now the one who was sown upon the rocky places is the one who hears the Word [of God] and immediately receives it with joy; but *because* he has no root in himself, *he* does not endure; for when tribulation or persecution arises because of the Word, he is quickly offended. And the one who was sown among the thorns is the one who hears the Word, but the cares of this life and the deceitfulness of riches choke the Word, and it becomes unfruitful.

"**But the one who was sown on good ground, this is the one who hears the Word** [the seed is the Word of God (Luke 8:10)] **and understands**, who indeed brings forth fruit and produces—one a hundredfold, another sixtyfold *and* another thirtyfold" (Matt. 13:16, 18-23).

After Jesus had spoken another parable about sowing the good seed and the tares, He dismissed the multitude. "Then His disciples came to Him, saying, 'Explain to us the parable of the tares of the field.' And He answered *and* said to them, 'The One Who sows the good seed is the Son of man; and **the field is the world; and the good seed, these are the children of the kingdom; but the tares are the children of the wicked *one*.**

" 'Now the enemy who sowed them is the devil; and **the harvest is *the* end of the age** [when Jesus returns], and the reapers are the angels. Therefore, as the tares are gathered and consumed in the fire, so shall it be in the end of this age. The Son of man shall send forth His angels, and they shall gather out of His kingdom all the offenders and those who are practicing lawlessness; and they shall cast them into the furnace of fire; there shall be weeping and gnashing of teeth. Then shall the righteous shine forth as the sun in the kingdom of their Father. **The one who has ears to hear, let him hear'** " (Matt. 13:36-43).

How Does God Call Us?

As Jesus said, "Many are called, but few are chosen." But *how* does God call us? Jesus commanded His apostles to go into all the world, to all nations (Matt. 28:18-20), even "to the ends of the earth" (Acts 1:8). However, all of the apostles *died* before reaching the "ends of the earth." On the other hand, reaching the "ends of the earth" *has been* and *is being* accomplished through the published Word of God—Old and New Testaments.

Jesus also prophesied that before the end of this age the Gospel would be preached and published in all the world. "And this gospel of the kingdom shall be **proclaimed** in all the world for a witness to all nations; and then shall the end come" (Matt. 24:14). Jesus also said, "And the gospel must first be **published** among all nations" (Mark 13:10).

Since these prophecies have been only *partially* fulfilled, the Gospel will continue to be proclaimed until Christ's return. Billions of people will yet be able to hear the witness of God. In fact, in the final days of this age, *everyone on earth* will receive the greatest witness of all time![5] But true to Jesus' words, only a *few* will heed the witness and answer God's call to repentance!

Let's examine some of the ways God calls a person today. The calling of God begins with the Word of God—when a person reads the Bible or hears the Scriptures being preached. It could be through a television program, a DVD or CD, or by listening to a radio program—or it could simply be through reading biblical articles, booklets or books. Moreover, a calling can be initiated when a person shares his or her Christian experience with a non-Christian.

Most often, God begins to call us when we are experiencing times of trouble, sickness, the death of a loved one, the loss of a job, or when we are disillusioned because everything seems to be going wrong. We experience problems, difficulties, and trials in our lives—we feel overwhelmed, at the end of our rope, even lost. We don't know what to do! At some point, we realize how *helpless* we really are!

When people are going through times like this, they often begin calling out to God. For many, crying out to God may be their very first prayer. God hears those prayers and will answer! He will intervene and bring relief, comfort, and give us peace in our minds and hearts. This is all a part of how God brings us to Christ (John 6:44).

This is what Jesus meant when He said, "**Ask**, and it shall be given to you. **Seek**, and you shall find. **Knock**, and it shall be opened to you. **For everyone who asks receives, and the one who seeks finds, and to the one who knocks it shall be opened**" (Matt. 7:7-8). This is what Jesus promised!

How Does God Know When We Begin to Seek Him? To most people, God is somewhere far away. Many even ask, "Does God really know I exist? How can He possibly know anything about me?"

But God is not far off! He declares that He is near: " '*Am* I a God *Who is* near,' says the LORD, 'and not a God afar off? Can anyone hide himself in secret places so that I shall not see him?' says the LORD. 'Do I not fill the heavens and *the* earth [all creation]?' says the LORD" (Jer. 23:23-24).

Obviously, God is *not* near to the wicked. However, He *is* near to those who call out to Him for help and seek Him with a repentant attitude. Here is how we are to seek God: "Seek the LORD while He may be found; **call upon Him while He is near. Let the wicked forsake his way, and the unrighteous man his thoughts; and let him return to the LORD, and He will have mercy upon him; and to our God, for He will abundantly pardon**" (Isa. 55:6-7).

We must turn to God with a *humble heart*. "**The LORD is near to the broken-hearted and saves those who are of a contrite spirit**" (Psa. 34:18). We must call out to God from the depths of our heart *in truth*. "**The

LORD **is near unto all who call upon Him, unto all who call upon Him in truth**. He will fulfill the desire of those who fear Him; He also will hear their cry, and will save them. **The LORD watches over all who love Him**, but all the wicked He will destroy" (Psa. 145:18-20).

Jesus and the Seven Spirits: Few people understand *how* God is able to watch over those who seek, obey and love Him, as well as, to know what the wicked are doing. The answer involves what Jesus calls the "seven spirits." John writes, "[To] the seven churches that *are* in Asia: Grace and peace *be* to you from Him Who is, and Who was, and Who *is* to come; and from **the seven spirits that are before His** [God's] **throne; and from Jesus Christ**, the faithful Witness, the Firstborn from the dead, and the Ruler of the kings of the earth…" (Rev. 1:4-5).

In His message to the church at Sardis, Jesus states that He *has*, or utilizes, the seven spirits of God. "These things says **He Who has the seven spirits of God** and the seven stars…" (Rev. 3:1). (The seven stars are the seven angels to the seven churches—Rev. 1:20).

When in vision, John was taken up to the very throne of God, **he also sees the seven spirits**. "After these things I looked, and behold, a door opened in heaven; and the first voice that I heard *was* as if a trumpet were speaking with me, saying, 'Come up here, and I will show you *the* things that must take place after these things.' And immediately I was in *the* Spirit; and behold, a throne was set in heaven, and *One was* sitting on the throne. And He Who *was* sitting was in appearance like a jasper stone and a sardius stone; and a rainbow *was* around the throne, like an emerald in its appearance.

"And around the throne *were* twenty-four thrones; and on the thrones I saw twenty-four elders sitting, clothed in white garments; and they had on their heads golden crowns. And proceeding from the throne were lightnings and thunders and voices; and seven lamps of fire, which are the **seven spirits of God**, *were* burning before the throne" (Rev. 4:1-5).

What is the purpose of the seven spirits? Why are they there? What do they do? We find the answer in Revelation five. As John continued looking at the throne of God, he wrote, "Then I saw, and behold, before the throne and the four living creatures, and before the elders, *was* standing a Lamb as having been slain [Jesus Christ], having seven horns [the seven churches of chapters 2 and 3] and **seven eyes, which are the <u>seven spirits of God</u> that are sent into all the earth**" (Rev. 5:6).

These seven spirits, used and controlled by Christ, are seven special "eyes" of God that are "sent into all the earth." Why are they sent into all the earth? What do they do?

The Old Testament prophet Zechariah saw a vision of the throne of God, which included a **lampstand with seven lamps**. When he inquired about the lamps, God told him, **"These seven are the eyes of the LORD which run to and fro through the whole earth"** (Zech. 4:10).

Why do they "run to and fro through the whole earth"? As we will see, God uses them to keep watch over the entire earth, including all the nations. This is how God can *know exactly* what is going on at all times. "He rules by His power forever; **His eyes keep watch upon the nations…**" (Psa. 66:7). This applies to individuals as well. "**For the eyes of the LORD run to and fro in all the whole earth** to show Himself strong on behalf of those whose heart *is* perfect toward Him" (II Chron. 16:9).

The following passage is similar to what John saw in Revelation: "The LORD is in His holy temple; the LORD'S throne is in heaven. **His eyes behold; His searching gaze tests the children of men**. The LORD tries the righteous, but His soul hates the wicked and the one who loves violence" (Psa. 11:4-5).

Thus, Jesus Christ, Who was the LORD God of the Old Testament, *uses* these seven "eyes"—which are constantly going throughout the whole world—to find those who are seeking Him (as well as those who are living wickedly). This is *how* He knows who is seeking God, and can thus hear their prayers. This is how God can *see* everything—good and evil: "**The eyes of the LORD are upon the righteous, and His ears are open to their cry.** <u>The face of the LORD is against those who do evil,</u> to cut off the memory of them from the earth. **The righteous cry, and the LORD hears, and delivers them out of all their troubles. The LORD is near to the brokenhearted and saves those who are of a contrite spirit**" (Psa. 34:15-18).

After God has answered our first prayers, we will begin to hunger and thirst for additional knowledge about God and Christ. Jesus will respond to us as He promised: "Blessed are those who hunger and thirst after righteousness, for they will be filled" (Matt. 5:6). When we come to Jesus, the spiritual "bread of life," we will be *filled*. He said, "I am the bread of life; the one who comes to Me shall never hunger; and the one who believes in Me shall never thirst at any time" (John 6:35). This is how we *answer* God's call—by drawing close to God and Christ.

As God draws us more and more—and as we yield to His will and repent of our sins—we begin to keep His commandments more fully. Ultimately, our desire is to be among those who are *chosen*.

How Does God Choose?

Now that we have seen that "many are called, but few are chosen," the question is, *How does God choose?* Since God has given us absolute independent free moral agency, the answer ultimately depends on *our response* to God's call to repent, believe the Gospel, and believe in Jesus as our personal Savior.

When people hear God's call and do *not* respond, it is often because they do not realize that they have sinned and need to repent. Sin is much greater than just having "done wrong"—and repentance is so much more than just "feeling sorry" for what one has done. *We must come to see ourselves inherently as sinners.* This proverb summarizes it well: "There is a way [of life and a way of thinking] which seems right to a man [he does not realize it is wrong], but the end [result] thereof *is* the way of death" (Prov. 14:12).

But what is sin? The apostle John gives us a clear biblical definition: "[For] sin is the transgression of the law" (I John 3:4; *KJV*). A literal translation brings out a much broader meaning: "Everyone who **practices sin is also practicing lawlessness, for sin is lawlessness.**" To "practice" sin means a person is living a life that is constantly and repeatedly transgressing the laws and commandments of God—in other words, habitually "practicing lawlessness" as a way of living. *Lawlessness* encompasses many things: to be against all law; to foster chaos and anarchy; to live without God's laws and commandments; to live with a mixture of some of God's laws and the traditions or teachings of men; or, to add to or take away from the laws and commandments of God. But the truth is, "all have sinned and come short of the glory of God."

So *how* and *when* does God "choose" a person?

The answer involves the work of God the Father—because the Father is directly involved in choosing, or selecting, those who answer Jesus' call to repentance. Moreover, Jesus made it clear that only He could *reveal* the Father to those called: "At that time Jesus answered and said, 'I praise You, O Father, Lord of heaven and earth, that You have hidden these things from the wise and intelligent, and have revealed them to babes. Yes, Father, for it was well pleasing in Your sight *to do* this. All things were delivered to Me by My Father; and **no one knows the Son except the Father; neither does anyone know the Father except the Son, and the one to whom the Son personally chooses to reveal *Him*'** " (Matt. 11:25-27; also see I Cor. 1:26-31).

Indeed, in order to come to the Father, one must come through Jesus: "I am the way, and the truth, and the life; **no one comes to the Father except through Me**" (John 14:6).

But Jesus also revealed that being chosen for eternal life involves the Father's initiative. Jesus explains: "**No one can come to Me unless the Father, Who sent Me, draws him**..." (John 6:44). Thus, God the Father draws people with His Spirit, leading them to repentance. As Romans 2:4

shows, it is the "graciousness of God" that leads us to repentance. In other words, repentance is by the grace of God, Who draws individuals to Christ. And one must continue to respond to the leading of God, or He will cease and withdraw His Spirit.

John writes about an occasion when many of Jesus' disciples left Him because they were offended at some of His teachings. When they departed, they turned their backs on God's call to eternal life. Instead of repenting and seeking to understand what Jesus was teaching, they left. Again, "many are called, but few are chosen." When those disciples left, God ceased to draw them and withdrew His Spirit. Thus, they were not *chosen* for eternal life.

To the disciples who remained, Jesus reiterated that to be *chosen* for eternal life is the joint action of God the Father and Himself: " 'But there are some of you who do not believe.' For Jesus knew from *the* beginning who were the ones that did not believe, and who would betray Him. And He said, 'For this reason, I have said to you, **no one can come to Me unless it has been given to him from My Father**.' From that *time*, many of His disciples went back and walked no more with Him. Therefore, Jesus said to the twelve, 'Are you also desiring to go away?' Then Simon Peter answered Him, '**Lord, to whom shall we go? You have the words of eternal life**' " (John 6:64-68).

Decades later, John wrote that there is no eternal life without both God the Father and Jesus the Christ: "I did not write to you because you do not know the truth, but because you know it, and *you understand* that not one lie comes from the truth. **Who is the liar if it is not the one who denies that Jesus is the Christ? He is the antichrist—the one who denies the Father and the Son. Anyone who denies the Son does not have the Father either**" (I John 2:21-23).

When a person truly repents of his or her past sins and accepts the shed blood of Jesus as full payment for those sins, it is necessary to then be baptized by full immersion in water. Under the New Covenant, water baptism symbolizes the *death* of the old sinful self. In baptism, God spiritually conjoins this symbolic death of the repentant sinner with Jesus' crucifixion and death. Through baptism, the new believer makes a solemn pledge to God to cease living in sin and to love God and keep His commandments as a way of life.

Paul makes this absolutely clear: "What then shall we say? Shall we continue in sin, so that grace may abound? MAY IT NEVER BE! **We who died to sin, how shall we live any longer therein**? Or are you ignorant that we, as many as were baptized into Christ Jesus, were baptized into His death?

"Therefore, we were buried with Him through the baptism into the death; so that, just as Christ was raised from *the* dead by the glory of the Father, in the same way, we also should walk in newness of life [loving God and keeping His commandments]. For if we have been conjoined together in the likeness of His death, so also shall we be *in the likeness* of *His* resurrection [the promise of eternal life].

"**Knowing this, that our old man was co-crucified with *Him* in order that the body of sin might be destroyed, so that we might no longer be enslaved to sin**; because the one who has died *to sin* has been justified from sin [all of one's sins have been forgiven]. Now if we died together with Christ, we believe that we shall also live with Him" (Rom. 6:1-8).

After being baptized, the elder or minister lays his hands on the head of the believer and prays to God the Father that he or she may receive the gift of the Holy Spirit (Acts 2:38; 8:15; 19:1-6). *Following baptism—upon receiving the Holy Spirit—the new believer is fully chosen by God the Father and Jesus Christ.*

In the next chapter we will see how the newly baptized believer is to live and walk in newness of life, as led by the Holy Spirit of God.

Chapter 9 Notes:

1. Today, there are almost *seven* billion Bibles in circulation covering every major language—that's nearly a Bible for every person on earth! In addition, there are multiple millions of digital Bibles used on a variety of electronic devices.

2. For a scriptural summary of true Christianity, please see "Beliefs and Doctrines of the New Testament Church" at www.cbcg.org/beliefs.htm.

3. Concerning false teachers and false prophets, see Matt. 24:11, 24; Mark 13:22; Acts 20:29-30; II Cor. 11:13-15; II Pet. 2:1-3; and I John 4:1.

4. Of the original apostles Jesus called and chose, it was Judas Iscariot who betrayed Him. He was later replaced by Matthias (Acts 1:26).

5. The greatest witness of the Gospel will yet come from the Two Witnesses and the three angels' messages (see Rev. 11:3-12; 14:6-11).

CHAPTER TEN

Rescued from Satan the Devil
to Walk in Newness of Life

Now that you have been saved from your sins through baptism, received the Holy Spirit, and been chosen by God, you have direct access to God the Father through your personal prayer and Bible study. Moreover, God has personally *rescued* you from Satan the devil—the author of sin! The apostle Paul states that the very purpose of his calling and ministry was to turn people from Satan, the "god of this world," to the true God and to Jesus the Christ. When he was called, Jesus gave him this mandate: " 'To open their eyes [those being called and chosen], that *they* may **turn from darkness to light, and *from* the authority of Satan to God**, so that they may receive remission of sins and an inheritance among those who have been sanctified [chosen] through faith in Me [Jesus]' " (Acts 26:18).

Christ said, "I am the light of the world; the one who follows Me shall never walk in darkness, but shall have the light of life" (John 8:12). Every true believer is to constantly come to Jesus, and practice, as a way of life, the truth of God: "And this is the judgment: that the light [Jesus] has come into the world, but men loved darkness rather than the light because their works were evil. For everyone who practices [and continues to practice] evil hates the light, and does not come to the light, so that his works may not be exposed; **but the one who practices** [and continues to practice] **the truth comes to the light, so that his works may be manifested, that they have been accomplished by *the power of* God**" (John 3:19-21).

In Jesus' final prayer to the Father just before He was arrested, He prayed for *all* of the disciples—including those who were to yet believe through the apostles' teachings: "**I am praying for them; I am not praying for the world, but for those whom You have given Me, for they are Yours.... I do not pray that You would take them out of the world, but that You would <u>keep</u> [protect] them from the evil one**" (John 17:9, 15).

There is no doubt that the Father continues to answer Jesus' prayer to *keep you* from the evil one—Satan the devil. But you are also involved—*you* are to pray that God will continue to rescue you from the evil one!

In the beginning of His ministry, Jesus taught His disciples to pray *directly* to God. In the model or outline of how to pray, He instructed them to begin with God the Father. Since they were not to give long public prayers, notice what Jesus taught them: "But you, **when you pray, enter into a private room**; and after shutting the door, pray to your Father Who *is* in secret; and your Father Who sees in secret shall reward you openly. **And when you pray, do not use vain repetitions, as the heathen *do*; for they think that by multiplying their words they shall be heard.**

"Now then, do not be like them; for your Father knows what things you have need of before you ask Him. Therefore, you are to pray after this manner [or according to this outline]: '**Our Father Who *is* in heaven, hallowed be Your name**; Your kingdom come; Your will be done on earth, as *it is* in heaven; give us this day our daily bread; and forgive us our debts, as we also forgive our debtors; **and lead us not into temptation, but <u>rescue us from the evil one</u>**. For Yours is the kingdom and the power and the glory forever. Amen' " (Matt. 6:6-13).

Only by the grace of God can you be saved from your sins and from Satan the devil. Before you answered God's call and were chosen, you were as good as dead in your sins. Paul explains: "Now you were dead in trespasses and sins, in which you walked in times past according to the course of this world, according to **the prince of the power of the air** [Satan the devil], **the spirit that is now working within the children of disobedience**; among whom also we all once had our conduct in the lusts of our flesh, doing the things willed by the flesh and by the mind, and were by nature *the* children of wrath, even as the rest *of the world*.

"But God, Who is rich in mercy, because of His great love with which He loved us, even when we were dead in *our* trespasses, has made *us* alive together with Christ. (*For* you have been saved [from your sins *and* Satan the devil] by grace.)" (Eph. 2:1-5).

In fact, it is God the Father Who personally does this for you: "Giving thanks to the Father, **Who has made us qualified for the share of the inheritance of the saints in the light; Who <u>has personally rescued us from the power of darkness</u> and has transferred *us* unto the kingdom of the Son of His love**; in Whom we have redemption through His own blood, *even* the remission of sins" (Col. 1:12-14).

Though the Father has personally rescued you from Satan, there will be times when the devil will try to tempt you and draw you away from God and your new life in Christ. When that happens, here is what you are to do: **"Therefore, submit yourselves to God. Resist the devil, and he will flee from you. Draw near to God, and He will draw near to you"** (James 4:7-8).

The apostle Peter also admonishes us on how to resist the wiles of Satan: "Be sober! Be vigilant! For your adversary *the* devil is prowling about as a roaring lion, seeking anyone he may devour. Whom **resist, steadfast in the faith**, knowing *that* the same afflictions are being fulfilled among your brethren who *are* in *the* world. Now may the God of all grace, **Who has called us unto His eternal glory in Christ Jesus**, after *you* have suffered a little while, Himself **perfect you, establish, strengthen,** *and* **settle** *you*. To Him *be* the glory and the power into the ages of eternity" (I Pet. 5:8-11).

When Jesus Himself was severely tempted by Satan for forty days and forty nights, He demonstrated exactly what you should do. You are to cast those thoughts and temptations out of your mind and rebuke the devil. Jesus fought Satan's temptations *by quoting Scripture* in answer to the devil's propositions. Notice here that when Jesus says "You" He is not referring to what Satan should do. Rather, He is referring to *Himself*, as a man—to what *He* should do. Jesus said to Satan: "It is written, 'Man shall not live by bread alone, but by every word that proceeds out of the mouth of God.' " And, "Again, it is written, 'You shall not tempt *the* Lord your God.' "

After that, the devil took Jesus to an exceedingly high mountain and showed Him all the kingdoms of the world and their glory. Satan said, "All these things will I give You, if You will fall down and worship me." Jesus responded, "**Begone, Satan!** For it is written [to everyone], 'You shall worship the Lord your God, and Him alone shall you serve.' " The devil then left Jesus alone (see Matt. 4:1-11).

God the Father and Jesus Christ will always hear and answer your prayers when you draw near to God and *resist* Satan by using the Word of God!

Once Chosen, You Are to Walk in Newness of Life

God chooses you at baptism when you receive the Holy Spirit. This is the beginning of your salvation and your new life in Christ. Every Christian is to live his or her life by doing or practicing the will of God. (Matt. 7:21). As Paul writes, since your sins have been buried in the watery grave of baptism, you are to live unto God and walk in newness of life through Jesus: "For when He [Jesus] died, He died unto sin once for all; but in that He lives, He lives unto God. In the same way also, you should indeed reckon yourselves to be **dead to sin**, but **alive to God** through Christ Jesus our Lord.

"**Therefore, do not let sin rule in your mortal body by obeying it in the lusts thereof** [as you did before baptism]. Likewise, do not yield your members as instruments of unrighteousness to sin; rather, **yield yourselves to God as those who are alive from** *the* **dead, and your members** *as* **instruments of righteousness to God**…. Don't you realize that to whom you yield yourselves *as* servants to obey, **you are servants of the one you obey,**

whether *it is* of sin unto death, or of obedience unto righteousness?

"But thanks *be* to God, that you were *the* servants of sin, but you have obeyed from *the* heart that form of doctrine which was delivered to you; and **having been delivered from sin, you became *the* servants of righteousness**" (Rom. 6:10-13, 16-18).

What is righteousness? Righteousness comes from God and you are to live your life in accord with the commandments of God. In Psalm 119, King David declared the righteousness of God: "**All Your commandments are righteousness**" (verse 172). "**Your righteousness is an everlasting righteousness**, and Your law is the truth…. Your commandments are my delight. **The righteousness of Your testimonies is everlasting**; give me understanding, and I shall live" (verses 142-144). "O LORD … all Your commandments are truth…. Your word is true from the beginning, and every one of Your righteous ordinances endures forever" (verses 151, 160).

Finally, David ties this together with the salvation of God. "Surely His salvation is near to those who fear Him…. **Mercy and truth have met together; righteousness and peace have kissed each other**" (Psa. 85:9-10).

***The Spiritual Seed of Abraham*:** When you are baptized and receive the Holy Spirit of God, you become part of the *spiritual* seed of Abraham and heirs according to the promise of eternal life. Paul makes this clear: "**For as many *of you* as were baptized into Christ did put on Christ**. There is neither Jew nor Greek; there is neither bond nor free; there is neither male nor female; for you are all one in Christ Jesus. **And if you *are* Christ's, then you are Abraham's seed, and heirs according to *the* promise**" (Gal. 3:27-29).

Abraham was given the promises because he "believed in the LORD. And He [God] counted it to him for righteousness" (Gen. 15:6). If you truly believe God, as did Abraham, then you will obey what God commands. Indeed, faith and belief are perfected by *obedience* (James 2:20-26). God declared to Isaac that he received the blessings of his father because "Abraham obeyed My voice and kept My charge, My commandments, My statutes, and My laws" (Gen. 26:5). Since you are now Abraham's seed, you are to follow his example of loving God and keeping His laws and commandments. John writes: "**For this is the love of God: that we keep His commandments; and His commandments are not burdensome**" (I John 5:3).

Now that you have been chosen by God and have received the Holy Spirit, you will begin to demonstrate a greater love for God—because you now belong to God! In fact, Jesus instructs you to *love God*, which is the "greatest commandment": "Jesus answered and said, 'You shall love *the* Lord your God with **all your heart**, and with **all your soul**, and with **all your mind**.' This is *the* first and greatest commandment; and *the* second *one is* like it: 'You shall love your neighbor as yourself.' **On these two commandments hang all the Law and the Prophets**" (Matt. 22:37-40).

There is no doubt that God the Father and Jesus Christ chose you because They love you. How then do you show your love for Them in return? Jesus told His disciples that love and commandment-keeping are bound together. "**If you love Me, keep the commandments—namely, My commandments**…. As the Father has loved Me, I also have loved you; live in My love. **If you keep My commandments, you shall live in My love; just as I have kept My Father's commandments and live in His love**…. The Father Himself loves you…" (John 14:15; 15:9-10; 16:27).

The Holy Spirit—the Love of God for You and Your Love for God

The Holy Spirit is the special spiritual power that God uses to create and accomplish His will.[1] During Jesus' final instructions to the apostles on the night of His last Passover, He spoke extensively about the Holy Spirit. As we will see, when you receive the gift of the Holy Spirit, it is actually the joint work of both the Father and Christ. Notice how Jesus explained it:

" 'If you love Me, keep the commandments—namely, My commandments. And I will ask the Father, and He shall give you another Comforter, that it may be with you throughout the age: *even* **the Spirit of the truth**, which the world cannot receive because it perceives it not, nor knows it; but you know it because **it dwells with you, and shall be within you**. I will not leave you orphans; I will come to you…. In that day, you shall know that I am in My Father, and you *are* in Me, and I am in you. **The one who has My commandments and is keeping them, that is the one who loves Me; and the one who loves Me shall be loved by My Father, and I will love him and will manifest Myself to him**.'

"Judas (not Iscariot) said to him, 'Lord, what has happened that You are about to manifest Yourself to us, and not to the world?' Jesus answered and said to him, '**If anyone loves Me, he will keep My word; and My Father will love him, and <u>We will come to him and make Our abode with him</u>**. The one who does not love Me does not keep My words; and the word that you hear is not Mine, but the Father's, Who sent Me' " (John 14:15-18, 20-24).

These are some of the most important verses in the New Testament. Jesus clearly says that sending the Holy Spirit is the joint spiritual work of God the Father and Christ. Notice: "But *when* the Comforter *comes, even* **the Holy Spirit, which <u>the Father will send in My name</u>**, that one shall teach you all things, and shall bring to your remembrance everything that I have told you…. But when the Comforter has come, **which I will send to you from the Father,** *even* **the Spirit of the truth, which proceeds from the Father**, that one shall bear witness of Me" (John 14:26; 15:26).

Thus, it is through the power of the Holy Spirit that God the Father and Jesus Christ spiritually dwell within each one who has been chosen. This is a great secret, or mystery, of God. Paul describes it this way: "That we [who are chosen] might be to *the* praise of His glory, who first trusted in the Christ; in Whom you also trusted after hearing the Word of the truth, the gospel of your salvation; in Whom also, after believing, **you were sealed with the Holy Spirit of promise, which is** *the* **earnest of our inheritance until** *the* **redemption of the purchased possession, to** *the* **praise of His glory**" (Eph. 1:12-14).

When you receive the Holy Spirit, it is actually the *earnest*, or down payment, of eternal life. It is at the first resurrection when Jesus returns that you—and all the "called, chosen and faithful" (Rev. 17:14)—will receive the *fullness* of eternal life. Until that time, you must continue to dwell in Jesus and the Father. Indeed, you are to be "growing [continuously] in *the* grace and *the* knowledge of our Lord and Savior Jesus Christ" (II Pet. 3:18).

Jesus explained this to His disciples by comparing Himself to a *vine* to which they were attached. At the same time, He emphasized that the Father actually *causes* the growth in spiritual character: "**I am the true vine, and My Father is the husbandman**. He takes away every branch in Me *that* does not bear fruit; but He cleanses each one that bears fruit, in order that it may bear more fruit. You are already clean through the word that I have spoken to you.

"Dwell in Me, and I in you. As a branch cannot bear fruit of itself, but only if it remains in the vine, neither *can* you *bear fruit* unless you are dwelling in Me. I am the vine, *and* you *are* the branches. **The one who is dwelling in Me, and I in him, bears much fruit; because apart from Me you can do nothing**. If anyone does not dwell in Me, he is cast out as a branch, and is dried up; and men gather them and cast *them* into a fire, and they are burned.

"**If you dwell in Me, and My words dwell in you**, you shall ask whatever you desire, and it shall come to pass for you. **In this is My Father glorified, that you bear much fruit; so shall you be My disciples**" (John 15:1-8).

Referring to the "greatest commandment," Jesus said you are to love God "with all your heart, and with all your soul, and with all your mind, and with all your strength" (Mark 12:30). This is made possible by the power of the Holy Spirit dwelling within you. "God is love"—and His love *toward you* is based on His love for Jesus and on Jesus' love for the Father. Thus, the *combined* love of God the Father and Jesus Christ is given to you.

In turn, through the Holy Spirit, you can love the Father and Christ with a more complete love. Looking again at John 15, Jesus next makes this profound statement: "**As the Father has loved Me** [Can there be any greater love than this?], **I also have loved you; <u>live in My love</u>**" (verse 9).

Living in the love of God is not just some emotional experience; it involves your whole being in devoted love and obedience to God in all things. Note carefully how Jesus explains it: "**IF you keep My commandments, you shall <u>live in My love</u>; just as I have kept My Father's commandments and <u>live in His love</u>**" (verse 10).

Continuing: "These things I have spoken to you, in order that My joy may dwell in you, and *that* your joy may be full: This is My commandment: that you love one another, as I have loved you. No one has greater love than this: that one lay down his life for his friends. You are My friends, if you do whatever I command you. No longer do I call you servants, because the servant does not know what his master is doing. But I have called you friends because I have made known to you all *the* things that I have heard from My Father.

"**You yourselves did not choose Me, but I have personally chosen you**, and ordained you, that you should go *forth* and bear fruit, and that your fruit should remain; so that whatever you shall ask the Father in My name, He may give you. These things I command you, that you love one another" (verses 11-17).

The Father Himself Loves You: Jesus then explains to the apostles that He would be going away—by dying and being buried. However, they would see Him again—after His resurrection. "And likewise, you indeed have grief now; but I will see you again, and your heart shall rejoice, and no one shall take your joy from you. And in that day [the day of His resurrection] you shall ask Me nothing. **Truly, truly I tell you, whatever you shall ask the Father in My name, He will give you**.

"Until this day, you have asked nothing in My name. Ask, and you shall receive, that your joy may be full. These things I have spoken to you in allegories; but the time is coming when I will no longer speak to you in allegories, but **I will plainly disclose to you *the things* of the Father**. In that day, you shall ask in My name; and I do not tell you that I will beseech the Father for you, for **the Father Himself loves you, because you have loved Me, and have believed that I came forth from God**" (John 16:22-27).

Think and meditate on this!

What wonderful love God the Father and Jesus Christ have for those who are *chosen* and *faithful*. Their awesome love is powerful and intimately personal! Jesus said that through the power of the Holy Spirit both He and the Father will *come and make Their abode with us* (John 14:23). Through Their love and the power of the Holy Spirit, *They dwell in you!* This stupendous divine relationship is the greatest thing that can happen in your life!

Think of it! Through prayer, you have personal, direct, unencumbered access to the great Sovereign Rulers of the universe—Who love you with supreme love! However, this wonderful fellowship you now have with God and Christ is only the down payment of your eternal life to come in the Family of God!

The truth is, God's ultimate purpose for all those who answer His call is so astounding and awe-inspiring that Jesus could not reveal it even to His apostles until years after He had ascended to heaven! He said, **"I have yet many things to tell you, but you are not able to bear them now. However, when that one has come,** *even* **the Spirit of the truth, it will lead you into all truth** because it shall not speak from itself, but whatever it shall hear, it shall speak. And it shall disclose to you the things to come" (John 16:12-13).

What were the things Jesus said He would yet reveal to His followers through the power of the Holy Spirit? As the next chapter will bring out, the answer has to do with astounding aspects of God's Master Plan of salvation. It involves understanding the "sonship of God"—the knowledge of how a person, who originally began human life in his or her mother's womb smaller than a speck of dust, can actually become a *son or daughter of God!*

Chapter 10 Note:

1. The Holy Spirit is the *power of God* by which He accomplishes His will. It is not a person or a third member of a so-called trinity. When the virgin Mary was impregnated by God the Father, He did so by the power of the Holy Spirit, just as the angel Gabriel had told her: *"The* Holy Spirit shall come upon you, and *the* **power of** *the* **Highest shall overshadow you**; and for this reason, the Holy One being begotten in you shall be called *the* Son of God" (Luke 1:35).

The Holy Spirit it is never called God. In the introduction to each of his epistles, the apostle Paul never acknowledges the Holy Spirit as God. Moreover, throughout the New Testament, the *neuter* gender Greek *to pneuma* (the spirit) is used exclusively.

The impregnation of the Holy Spirit from God the Father as a spiritual begettal and is granted freely to each believer upon repentance of sins, baptism by immersion, and the laying on of hands. This begettal of the Holy Spirit is the earnest and assurance of the promise of eternal life through Christ. It is the power of God, which makes each begotten child of God a partaker of the divine nature and imparts the ability to develop the love of God. The fruits of the Holy Spirit are love, joy, peace, longsuffering, gentleness, goodness, faith, meekness, and self-control. The indwelling of the Holy Spirit imparts the power to each individual to live in accordance with God's will and to overcome the temptations of human nature, the world, and Satan. As the spiritually begotten believer seeks to serve and obey God the Father and Jesus Christ, the Holy Spirit will lead him or her into all truth that is contained in the Word of God and is essential for salvation.

CHAPTER ELEVEN

A Later Revelation:
The Sonship of God

On the night of Jesus' last Passover, He told His apostles, "**I have yet many things to tell you, but you are not able to bear them now**. However, when that one has come, *even* the Spirit of the truth, it will lead you into all truth because it shall not speak from itself, but whatever it shall hear, it shall speak. **And it shall disclose to you the things to come**" (John 16:12-13). *Why* were the apostles not able to receive or understand certain truths at that time? *What* was Jesus going to reveal to them later through the power of the Holy Spirit?

In order to answer these questions, we need to go back and look at something Jesus told the disciples on His last trip to Jerusalem. Luke writes that He warned them what was about to happen: "And after taking the twelve *aside* to *Himself*, He said to them, 'Behold, we are going up to Jerusalem, and all things that have been written about the Son of man by the prophets shall be fulfilled. For He shall be delivered up to the Gentiles, and shall be mocked and insulted and spit upon. And after scourging *Him*, they shall kill Him; but on the third day, He shall rise again.' **But they understood none of these things, and this saying was hidden from them, and they did not comprehend what was said**" (Luke 18:31-34).

Later, when everything happened to Jesus exactly as He had said it would, the apostles were completely devastated and traumatized. They did not understand why Jesus had to *die*—let alone die such a cruel, gruesome death. Since they knew Jesus was the Messiah, it is likely that they had looked for Him to raise up an army and deliver Judea from Roman occupation—as well as set up the Kingdom of God at that time. But now that Jesus was dead, they were afraid of the Jewish authorities—fearing that they would likewise be arrested and killed.

After Jesus was resurrected from the dead, He suddenly appeared to the disciples. John writes: "Afterwards [after Jesus was in the tomb for three days and three nights and was raised from the dead], as evening was drawing near that day, the first *day* of the weeks, and the doors were shut where the disciples had assembled for fear of the Jews, Jesus came and stood in the midst, and said to them, 'Peace *be* to you.' And after saying this, He showed them His hands and His side. Then the disciples rejoiced *because* they had seen the Lord" (John 20:19-20).

That Jesus had been raised from the dead and was living again was absolutely startling—unbelievable! It was beyond their wildest expectations!

Luke provides additional details about Jesus' dramatic appearance to the disciples, who were hiding behind closed doors. As if coming out of nowhere, Jesus suddenly appeared. In His resurrected state, He must have walked *through* the door, or one of the walls, without even causing the slightest sound: "Now as they [two disciples with whom Jesus walked to Emmaus] were telling these things [that they had seen Jesus and even ate with Him], *then* Jesus Himself [suddenly] stood in their midst and said to them, 'Peace *be* to you.' But **they were terrified and filled with fear**, thinking *that* they beheld a [demonic] spirit *apparition*.

"Then He said to them, 'Why are you troubled? And why do doubts come up in your hearts? See My hands and My feet, that it is I. Touch Me and see *for yourselves*; for a [demon] spirit does not have flesh and bones, as you see Me having.' And after saying this, He showed them *His* hands and *His* feet. But while **they were still disbelieving and wondering for joy**, He said to them, 'Do you have anything here to eat?' Then they gave Him part of a broiled fish and a *piece* of honeycomb. And He took these *and* ate in their presence.

"And He said to them, '**These *are* the words that I spoke to you when I was yet with you, that all *the* things which were written concerning Me in the Law of Moses and *in the* Prophets and *in the* Psalms must be fulfilled.**' **Then He opened their minds to understand the Scriptures**, and said to them, 'According as it is written, it was necessary for the Christ to suffer, and to rise from *the* dead the third day. And in His name, repentance and remission of sins should be preached to all nations, beginning at Jerusalem" (Luke 24:36-47).

In the Book of Acts, Luke writes that after Jesus' resurrection He continued with them for an additional 40 days: "The first account I indeed have written, O Theophilus, concerning all things that Jesus began both to do and to teach, until the day in which He was taken up, after giving command by *the* Holy Spirit to the apostles whom He had chosen; to whom also, **by many infallible proofs, He presented Himself alive after He had suffered, being seen by them for forty days**, and speaking [and teaching] the things concerning the kingdom of God" (Acts 1:1-3). After the 40 days, Jesus ascended into heaven (Acts 1:9-11).

Apparently, what Jesus revealed to the apostles during this 40-day period was *not* what He had promised to ultimately reveal to them through the Holy Spirit. But, *what knowledge* was so profound that Jesus could not reveal it to His apostles even during those 40 days? *Why* were they not able to bear such knowledge at that time? As we will see, what Jesus would later reveal would be some of the deepest mysteries of God!

Twenty-six years after Jesus had ascended into heaven to sit at the right hand of God, Paul gives us some insight on how to understand the "deep things" of God: "Now we speak wisdom among the *spiritually* mature; however, *it is* not *the* wisdom of this world, nor of the rulers of this world, who are coming to nothing. Rather, **we speak *the* wisdom of God in a mystery, *even* the hidden *wisdom* that God foreordained before the ages unto our glory**, which not one of the rulers of this world has known (for if they had known, they would not have crucified the Lord of glory).

"But according as it is written, '*The* eye has not seen, nor *the* ear heard, neither have entered into *the* heart of man, *the* things which God has prepared for those who love Him.' **But God has revealed *them* to us by His Spirit, for the Spirit searches all things—even the deep things of God**. For who among men understands the things of man except *by* the spirit of man which *is* in him? **In the same way also, the things of God no one understands except *by* the Spirit of God**.

"Now we have not received the spirit of the world, but **the Spirit that *is* of God, so that we might know the things graciously given to us by God; which things we also speak, not in words taught by human wisdom, but in *words* taught by *the* Holy Spirit *in order to* communicate spiritual things by spiritual *means*.** But *the* natural man does not receive **the things of the Spirit of God**; for they are foolishness to him, and he cannot understand *them* because they **are spiritually discerned**" (I Cor. 2:6-14).

Before Jesus could reveal certain "deep things" of God to the apostles, they would need more time and experience preaching the Gospel and a better understanding of the Word of God (Acts 6:4, 7). Moreover, they would need more experience using the power of the Holy Spirit. Only when the time was right would Jesus reveal the ultimate secret or mystery of God. As we will see, this revelation answers the question, *Why were you born?*

The Sonship of God

Jesus' revelation of the "deep things" of God centers on what the apostle Paul calls the "sonship" of God. What is the *sonship* of God? As we will see, it is actually part of the original promise God made to Abraham concerning *the spiritual seed*: "And if you *are* Christ's [called and chosen], then you are Abraham's seed, and heirs according to *the* promise.... But when the time for the fulfillment came, God sent forth His own Son, born of a woman ... so that we might receive **the *gift of* sonship *from God*.** And because you are sons, God has sent forth the Spirit of His Son into your hearts, crying, 'Abba, Father' " (Gal. 3:29; 4:4-6).

Instead of using the word *sonship*, the *King James Version* translates the Greek *uiothesia* as "adoption." Unfortunately, this is an inadequate translation and clouds the meaning of what Paul is trying to convey. Indeed, *uiothesia* means *sonship*—referring to our *relationship* to God the Father—with no distinction between male or female. This is why we are to call God our *Father*, and even use the endearing term *Abba*, which in English means *daddy*. Such terminology clearly demonstrates the family nature of God.

This *sonship* of God begins when you are chosen and receive the Holy Spirit at baptism. Jesus revealed to His apostles that the power of the Holy Spirit would be within them. He explicitly said that He and the Father would *jointly* send the Holy Spirit. Through the "earnest" of the Holy Spirit, both Jesus and the Father would dwell within each person who is called and chosen (John 14:15-17; 14:26; 15:26).

In writing to the Romans, Paul states that those who do *not* have the Holy Spirit within them are counted by God as being "in the flesh." However, those who *do* have the Holy Spirit within them are reckoned as being "in the Spirit." Paul also emphasizes that the Holy Spirit is from *both* the Father and the Son. Both aspects of the Holy Spirit are necessary in order to belong to God, receive the sonship of God, and have eternal life: "For those who walk according to the flesh mind the things of the flesh; but those who walk according to *the* Spirit mind the things of the Spirit. For to be carnally minded *is* death, but to be spiritually minded *is* life and peace, because the carnal mind *is* enmity against God, for it is not subject to the law of God; neither indeed can it *be*. But those who are in *the* flesh cannot please God.

"However, you are not in *the* flesh, but in *the* Spirit, **if *the* Spirit of God** is indeed dwelling within you. But **if** anyone does not have ***the* Spirit of Christ**, he does not belong to Him. But **if Christ *be* within you**, the body *is* indeed dead because of sin; however, **the Spirit *is* life** because of righteousness. Now **if the Spirit of Him** [God the Father] **Who raised Jesus from *the* dead is dwelling within you**, He Who raised Christ from *the* dead will also quicken your mortal bodies because of **His Spirit that dwells within you**.

"So then, brethren, we are not debtors to the flesh, to live according to *the* flesh; because **if** you are living according to *the* flesh, you shall die; but **if by *the* Spirit** you are putting to death the deeds of the body, you shall live.

"**For as many as are led by *the* Spirit of God, these are *the* sons of God**. Now you have not received a spirit of bondage again unto fear, but

you have received *the* Spirit of sonship, whereby we call out, 'Abba, Father.' **The Spirit itself bears witness conjointly with our own spirit, *testifying* that we are *the* children of God**. Now **if** *we are* **children**, *we are* also heirs—truly, heirs of God and joint heirs with Christ—**if indeed we suffer together with Him, so that we may also be glorified together with Him**" (Rom. 8:5-17).

Notice that there are eight *conditional **IF** clauses*. Four pertain to God and His Spirit, and four pertain to each person who has the Holy Spirit. These show just how much your life and your choices are involved in your relationship with the Father and Christ. Moreover, your very *sonship* of God is accomplished through the power of the Holy Spirit!

It is revealing to note that there are no passages in the Gospels that directly relate to the sonship of God for those who are called and chosen. Only Jesus' begettal by God the Father via the Holy Spirit conveyed that such a relationship was possible. Thus, this special knowledge had to be divinely revealed. It was the reality of this *father-son relationship—the sonship of God*—that Jesus was waiting to reveal to the apostles—when they were able to bear it.

The Sonship of God Begins
When You Receive the Holy Spirit

Your human life began with *begettal*, the impregnation of one of your mother's ova by a sperm cell from your father. At that instant, the genes and chromosomes from your father and mother united, as God simultaneously *gave you life* by giving you the "spirit of man." This was your beginning as a person—an almost invisible speck of life in your mother's womb. Through the power of God, you were physically formed in the *image* and *likeness* of God. Finally, following your development in the womb, you were born into the human family!

An almost exact *parallel* exists between the begettal of new human life and the beginning of your spiritual life through the Holy Spirit. When you are baptized and receive the Holy Spirit, you are spiritually *begotten* by God. This is the beginning of your sonship—with God as your Father!

At your physical begettal you received the *spirit of man* from God. It was united with your brain, giving you the capacity to think, create, and have self-awareness. It also *gave you life*. It is precisely the same when the Father puts His Holy Spirit within you at baptism. At that instant, the Holy Spirit from God *unites* with your "spirit of man." This is the *beginning* of your spiritual life and your conversion. Paul describes it this way: "Now you have not received a spirit of bondage again unto fear [the spirit of this world], but **you have received** *the* **Spirit of sonship**, whereby we call out, 'Abba, Father.' The Spirit itself bears witness conjointly [that is, *united*] with our own spirit, *testifying* **that we are** *the* **children of God**" (Rom. 8:15-16).

Similar to human begettal, the receiving of the Holy Spirit is a *begettal* by God the Father—as He engenders new *spiritual life* in the spirit of your mind. In fact, Peter states that at this point you are "*begotten again*." He writes: "Peter, an apostle of Jesus Christ, to *the* **elect strangers** scattered in Pontus, Galatia, Cappadocia, Asia, and Bithynia; *who have been chosen* according to *the* predetermined knowledge of God *the* Father, **by sanctification through** *the* **Spirit**, unto obedience and sprinkling of *the* blood of Jesus Christ: Grace and peace be multiplied to you.

"**Blessed** *be* **the God and Father of our Lord Jesus Christ**, Who, according to His abundant mercy, **has begotten us again** unto a living hope through *the* resurrection of Jesus Christ from *the* dead; unto an inheritance incorruptible and undefiled and unfading, reserved in heaven for us" (I Pet. 1:1-4). When you receive the Holy Spirit, you are *spiritually begotten*. Peter says "again" because you had already been begotten in your mother's womb.

The apostle John confirms what Peter has written: "Everyone who believes that Jesus is the Christ [and has been baptized] **has been begotten by God**; and everyone who loves Him [God the Father] Who begat, also loves him who **has been begotten by Him** [that is, other begotten Christians]" (I John 5:1).

John further describes this *spiritual begettal* by drawing a parallel between the physical begettal of human life and the spiritual begettal of one's mind: "**Everyone who has been begotten by God** does not practice [live in] sin, because **His** [God the Father's] **seed** *of begettal* [the Holy Spirit] **is dwelling within him**, and he is [thus] not able to *practice* sin because **he has been begotten by God**" (I John 3:9). The Greek phrase "seed *of begettal*" comes from the Greek *sperma*—the root for the English word *sperm*. This fact reinforces the amazing parallel between human begettal and the spiritual begettal from God the Father via the Holy Spirit placed within each newly baptized believer!

Salvation Is a New Spiritual Creation

Newly begotten believers are to walk in *newness* of life as led by the Holy Spirit of God. This is the beginning of a life-long process of growing in the grace and the knowledge of our Lord, Jesus Christ (II Pet. 3:18). Just as a newly begotten baby in its mother's womb is not instantaneously ready for birth, newly begotten Christians are likewise not immediately ready to be *born again*.[1] Rather, the new believer must *grow* and *develop* spiritually before he or she is ready for the resurrection and eternal life at Jesus' return. This *process* requires life-long faithfulness.

As you begin your new walk in righteousness, you must learn to develop the spiritual obedience, love, and character that God requires in order for Him to *complete* His sonship within you. Paul shows that your sonship is a *new creation* in Christ: "**Therefore, if anyone** *be* **in Christ,** *he is* **a new creation**; the old things [the old way of living in sin] have passed away [buried through baptism]; behold, all things have become new [your new way of life]" (II Cor. 5:17). This "new creation" is the *process* of salvation. As Paul taught the Corinthians, "Now I am declaring to you, brethren, **the** *same* **gospel** that I proclaimed to you, which you also received, *and* **in which you are now standing; by which** <u>**you are also being saved**</u>, if you are holding fast *the* words that I proclaimed to you…" (I Cor. 15:1-2; also see 1:18).

The phrase "you are being saved" demonstrates that becoming a new creation in Christ is a life-long spiritual process. God the Father is saving you *through* Jesus, by His spiritual work within you. Paul writes: "For by grace[2] you have been saved through faith, and this *especially* is not of your own selves; *it is* the gift of God, not of [your own] works, so that no one may boast. **For we are** <u>**His workmanship, being created in Christ Jesus**</u> **unto** *the* **good works that God ordained beforehand in order that we might walk in them**" (Eph. 2:8-10).

As we analyze these all-important verses, we learn:

1. Those who have the Holy Spirit within them are "*being* saved"— because salvation is a *process*, the inner spiritual work of God the Father.
2. Works originating from one's *own self*, apart from God, cannot save.
3. The good works we are to have are those foreordained by God, as found in the Bible.
4. We are the workmanship of God—as He creates in us the character of Jesus.
5. We are to walk in the *way of life* found in the Scriptures, being faithful for the rest of our lives.

In this process of salvation, we are being "created in Christ Jesus." This ongoing spiritual creation taking place within us requires our active, full-time *participation*. The Holy Spirit empowers us to grow in grace and knowledge as we overcome the old self and our old way of living in sin. "If indeed you have heard Him and have been taught in Him, according to *the* truth in Jesus **that concerning your former conduct, you put off the old** man, which is corrupt according to deceitful lusts; and that you be <u>re-newed in the spirit of your mind</u>; and that you <u>put on the new man,</u> which according to God is <u>created in righteousness and holiness of the truth</u>" (Eph. 4:21-24).

Salvation Requires Active Faith *and* Works

The apostle James, the half-brother of Jesus, declares that **godly works coupled with faith brings perfection**: "<u>[F]aith, if it does not have works, is dead, by itself</u>. But someone is going to say, 'You have faith, and I have works.' *My answer is:* You prove your faith to me through your works, and I will prove my faith to you through my works. Do you believe that God is one? You do well *to believe this*. Even the demons believe—and tremble *in fear*" (James 2:17-19). Another way of stressing the faith-works connection is this: *You always act on what you believe.* Indeed, everyone has some kind of *faith* or *belief* system—as reflected by their works: what they think, what they say, what they do, and how they live.

James continues: "But are you willing to understand, O foolish man, that **faith without works is dead**? Was not Abraham our father [those who are Christ's are Abraham's spiritual seed] justified by works when he offered up Isaac, his own son, upon the altar? Do you not see that **faith was working together with his works, and by works *his* faith was perfected**? And the scripture was fulfilled which says, 'Now Abraham believed God, and it was reckoned to him for righteousness; and he was called a friend of God.'

"You see, then, that a man is **justified by works, and not by faith only**.... For as the body without *the* spirit is dead, in the same way also, faith without works is dead" (James 2:20-24, 26).

The key is this: When we love God and keep His commandments, we are not doing our *own* works; rather, we are doing the works God has given to us to do. Therefore, they are *His* works, not our own works. Furthermore, by doing works foreordained by *God*, we are not attempting to "save ourselves." We are not attempting to *earn* salvation through our own works, or through religious traditions and rituals.

In Jesus' personal messages to the seven churches of Revelation, He dogmatically states 12 times: "I know your works" (Rev. 2-3). Moreover, Jesus declares that He judges them *for their works*—by what they do. If their works are the *works of God* based on love and obedience, He commends them. But if their works are their *own* (or are inspired by Satan), He warns and corrects them, calling on them to *repent* of such works or lose salvation!

Finally, Jesus admonishes the churches to *keep His works* to the end: "But hold fast what you have until I come. And to **the one who overcomes, and keeps My works unto *the* end**, I will give authority over the nations; and he shall shepherd them with an iron rod, as vessels of pottery are broken in pieces; as I have also received from My Father.... The one who has an ear, let him hear what the Spirit says to the churches" (Rev. 2:25-27, 29).

In the same way, Paul warned the Corinthians that they were *not* to go back and embrace a sinful lifestyle. They were not to think that since they had been "saved" such behavior was acceptable to God. The reality is this: Since God has given us His Holy Spirit and dwells in us, He will not condone compromises with sin under any circumstances! We are not to mix sin with godliness!

Notice how strongly Paul exhorts the Corinthian to cease compromising with sin: "Do not be unequally yoked with unbelievers. For what do righteousness and lawlessness *have* in common? And what fellowship *does* light *have* with darkness? And what union *does* Christ *have* with Belial? Or what part *does* a believer *have* with an unbeliever?

"And what agreement *is there between* a temple of God and idols? For you are a temple of *the* living God [because of the Spirit of God in them], exactly as God said: '**I will dwell in them and walk in *them*; and I will be their God, and they shall be My people. <u>Therefore, come out from the midst of them and be separate</u>**,' says *the* Lord, 'and touch not *the* unclean, and I will receive you; and **I shall be a Father to you, and you shall be My sons and daughters**,' says *the* Lord Almighty. Now then, beloved, since we have these promises, **we should purge ourselves from every defilement of *the* flesh and *the* spirit, perfecting holiness in *the* fear of God**" (II Cor. 6:14-18; 7:1).

Paul likewise admonished the Galatians, who, instead of walking by the Spirit, growing in grace and knowledge, loving God, and keeping His commandments, were reverting back to carnal works of the flesh. In so doing they were wavering in their faithfulness: "**Now *this* I say, walk by *the* Spirit, and you will not fulfill the lust of the flesh**. For the flesh lusts against the Spirit, and the Spirit against the flesh; and these things are opposed to each other, so that you cannot do those things you wish to do" (Gal. 5:16-17).

Paul then strongly warns that those who practice carnal, fleshly ways will not inherit the Kingdom of God nor receive eternal life: "Now the works of the flesh are manifest, which are *these*: adultery, fornication, uncleanness, licentiousness, idolatry, witchcraft, hatred, strifes, jealousies, indignations, contentions, divisions, sects, envyings, murders, drunkenness,

revelings, and such things as these; concerning which **I am telling you beforehand, even as I have also said in the past, that those who do**
[practice] **such things shall not inherit** *the* **kingdom of God**" (verses 19-
21).

In contrast, the apostle encourages the Galatians to use the Spirit of God
to produce the fruits of godliness—the good works God had foreordained:
"**But the fruit of the Spirit is love, joy, peace, long-suffering, kindness,
goodness, faith, meekness, self-control; against such things there is no
law**. But those who *are* Christ's have crucified the flesh with its passions
and lusts. **If we live by** *the* **Spirit, we should also be walking by** *the* **Spirit**" (verses 22-25).

Keeping the commandments of God is not easy, because doing so is
contrary to human nature and the way of the world. However, by being led
by the Spirit of God—instead of being led by personal lust—you can endure
and develop godly character, even in difficult times. Paul writes:
"Therefore, having been justified by faith, we have peace with God through
our Lord Jesus Christ. Through Whom **we also have access by faith into
this grace in which we stand**, and we ourselves boast in *the* hope of the
glory of God. And not only *this*, but we also boast in tribulations, realizing
that **tribulation brings forth endurance, and endurance** *brings forth*
character, and character *brings forth* **hope**. And the hope *of God* never
makes us ashamed because the love of God has been poured out into our
hearts through the Holy Spirit, which has been given to us" (Rom. 5:1-5).
As Jesus promised, "the one who endures to *the* end, that one shall be
saved" (Matt. 24:13). Thus, faithfulness is a life-long process.

Repentance and Forgiveness

Though you may stumble and fall spiritually (because of lust, weakness
of the flesh, or negligence), God will forgive you through His grace and the
blood of Christ—*if* you truly repent. You will be restored and reconciled to
the Father. John explains: "However, if we walk in the light, as He is in the
light, *then* we have fellowship with one another, and **the blood of Jesus
Christ, His own Son, cleanses us from all sin**. If we say that we do not
have sin, we are deceiving ourselves, and the truth is not in us.

"**If we confess our own sins, He is faithful and righteous, to forgive
us our sins, and to cleanse us from all unrighteousness**. If we say that we
have not sinned, we make Him a liar, and His Word is not in us. My little
children, I am writing these things to you so that you may not sin. And *yet*,
**if anyone does sin, we have an Advocate with the Father; Jesus Christ
the Righteous; and He is *the* propitiation for our sins; and not for our**

sins only, but also for *the sins of* the whole world" (I John 1:7-10; 2:1-2).

John emphasizes that keeping the commandments of God is a vital part of the spiritual *works* that God requires of every true believer. As we have seen, **if you are keeping the commandments of God as led by the Holy Spirit, then you are not doing your** *own* **personal works; rather, these are the "good works" that God has ordained for you to walk in**. Since God is not creating robots, He requires the full, *active participation* of those graciously granted sonship status. Your active love and obedience to God facilitates His spiritual workmanship of creating within you the love and righteousness of God for eternal life.

John writes: "**And by this** *standard* **we know that we know Him: if we keep His commandments**. The one who says, 'I know Him,' and does not keep His commandments, is a liar, and the truth is not in him. On the other hand, *if* **anyone is keeping His Word, truly** <u>in this one the love of God is being perfected</u>. By this *means* we know that we are in Him. **Anyone who claims to dwell in Him is obligating himself also** <u>to walk even as He Himself walked</u>" (I John 2:3-6).

Clearly, John is demonstrating that true Christian behavior is based on loving God, keeping His commandments, and walking as Jesus Himself walked. This is how every converted believer is being *perfected* in spiritual character—via the personal workmanship of the Father!

It takes *faith* to keep the commandments of God. In Revelation, we find this description of true Christians in the end time: "Here is *the* patience of the saints; here *are* **the ones who keep the commandments of God and the faith of Jesus**" (Rev. 14:12). When you think about it, it takes no faith at all to disobey God and reject His commandments. Thus, faith and keeping the commandments go hand in hand.

As you grow in grace and knowledge, developing the character of God through the Holy Spirit, God is creating *in you* the sonship of God: "My little children, we should not love in word, nor with *our* tongues; rather, *we should love* in deed and in truth. And in this *way* we know that we are of the truth, and shall assure our hearts before Him, that if our hearts condemn us [because we have sinned], God is greater than our hearts, and knows all things. Beloved, if our hearts do not condemn us [because we repent of our sins], *then* we have confidence toward God.

"And whatever we may ask we receive from Him because **we keep His commandments and practice those things that are pleasing in His sight**. And this is His commandment: that we believe on the name of His Son Jesus Christ, and that we love one another, exactly as He gave commandment to us. **And the one who keeps His commandments is dwelling in Him,** and He in him; and by this we know that He is dwelling in us: by the Spirit which He has given to us" (I John 3:18-24).

In the next chapter, we will examine God's final revelation to the apostles. This fantastic revelation unveils the magnitude of the *ultimate destiny* of those who have received the Father's sonship.

Chapter 11 Notes:

1. *What does it mean to be "born again"?* Being "born again" is perhaps one of the most misunderstood doctrines of the New Testament. The foremost reason is the erroneous insertion of words into the Latin translation of John 3, which completely distorts the original meaning as to *when* believers are "born again." The translation of key verses in John 3 from the 1380 Latin Vulgate by Wycliffe and the 1582 translation of the Rheims reads:

Wycliffe: "born again" (verses 3, 7); "born" (verses 4, 6 and 7); "born **again of water**" (verse 5)

Rheims: "born again" (verses 3, 7); "born" (verses 4, 6 and 7); "born **again of water**" (verse 5)

When compared to the original Greek, the word "again" has been *inserted* between "born" and "of water." The word "again" before "of water" is not in the original Greek text and should not have been added to the Latin text, which was carried over into these early English translations. This insertion was based on the assumption that a person is "born again" through water baptism.

However, that is not the case, as Jesus explained to Nicodemus: "Jesus answered and said to him, 'Truly, truly I say to you, **unless anyone is born again**, he cannot see the kingdom of God.' Nicodemus said to Him, 'How can a man who is old be born? Can he enter his mother's womb a second time and be born?' Jesus answered, 'Truly, truly I say to you, **unless anyone has been born of water and of Spirit**, he cannot enter the kingdom of God. That which has been **born of the flesh is flesh**; and that which has been **born of the Spirit is spirit**' " (John 3:3-6).

Jesus makes the direct parallel between being "born of water" and being "born of Spirit," which is this: When a physical baby is born of his/her mother, that is the birth of water, because the amniotic water of the birth sack combined with the mother's contractions causes the birth of a fleshly infant. Therefore, being "born of water" is being "born of the flesh"—wherein one is *composed* of "flesh." *This is one's first birth.*

Paul further makes it clear that "flesh and blood cannot see the kingdom of God" (I Cor. 15:50). Thus, it is impossible that baptism is a "born again" experience, because after baptism one is still a fleshly being. As a human being composed of flesh, no one can inherit the Kingdom of God. Moreover, Jesus clearly states that it is impossible for a person to see the Kingdom of God unless one has been "born again."

It is clear that Jesus was not talking about a conversion or baptismal experience in this dialogue. Rather, he was comparing one's physical birth—a fleshly existence—to that of being born anew or born again—to an actual spiritual existence. Jesus describes two births, one of water and one of the spirit—"unless anyone has been **born of water** and **of Spirit**" (John 3:5). Jesus then contrasts a birth of the flesh with a birth of the Spirit: "That which has been **born of the flesh is flesh**; and that which has been **born of the Spirit is spirit**" (John 3:6).

Physical Birth: When a human being is born, he or she is born of flesh—a physical being. Further, every human being has been "born of water" from the womb. **The one who has been born of water has been born of the flesh, and is flesh** (John 3:5-6).

Spiritual Birth: Nicodemus missed the point when Jesus referred to a new or second birth of the Spirit: "**unless anyone has been born ... of Spirit**." What kind of existence does one have who has been born of the Spirit? Jesus answered that question when He said "that which has been **born of the Spirit is spirit**." Jesus clearly meant that **anyone who has been born of the Spirit is, in fact, a spirit being**. The new, spiritual birth means that one who has been born again *is* a spirit being, no longer composed of human flesh. Since one who has been "born of the flesh is flesh," it follows, as Jesus said, that one who has been "born of the Spirit is spirit" (John 3:6).

Every human is limited by fleshly existence and the physical environment. However, as a spirit being, one is not bound by the flesh or limited by the physical realm. Jesus stated that one who has been "born of the Spirit" cannot necessarily be seen, just as the wind cannot be seen. He said: "**The wind blows where it wills**, and you hear its sound, but you do not know *the place* from which it comes and *the place* to which it goes; **so *also* is everyone who has been born of the Spirit**" (verse 8). Therefore, one who has been "born again"—"born of the Spirit"—must be invisible to the human eye, having the ability to come and go as the wind. That is hardly the case of one who has been baptized and converted; he or she is still in the flesh and is limited by the flesh—subject to death. Jesus said that a fleshly human being "cannot see" or "enter into" the Kingdom of God (John 3:3, 5; I Cor. 15:50).

When Is One Actually Born Again? Since one is not "born again" at baptism or conversion, *when* is one literally born again or born anew? It is through the birth, life, death, and resurrection of Jesus Christ that the New Testament reveals when a person is "born again." Matthew wrote that Jesus was the "firstborn" of the Virgin Mary (Matt. 1:25). Jesus' human birth was by water. He was flesh (I John 4:1-2), as any other human being, but He was "God manifested in *the* flesh" (I Tim. 3:16).

When Jesus was resurrected from the dead *as a spirit Being*, He was the "firstborn from the dead" (Col. 1:18; Rev. 1:4). Therefore, Jesus was "born again"—"born of the Spirit"—at the time He was resurrected. It was exactly as He had told Nicodemus, "That which has been born of the Spirit **is spirit**."

For a full discussion, please see Appendix 6, *What Does It Mean to Be "Born Again" or "Born of God"?*

2. Grace is the *free* and undeserved *gift* of God the Father through Jesus Christ. The grace of God is the greatest expression of the Father's love and all-encompassing mercy.

But grace is more than the forgiveness of sins. To be "under grace" means to be *continually* receiving God's divine love, favor, blessing, gracious care, help, goodwill, benefits, gifts, and goodness. God the Father is the *source* from which grace comes to the believer. The *only means* by which grace is granted to the believer is through the birth, life, crucifixion, death, and resurrection of Jesus as the perfect sacrifice of God. The believer enters the grace of God through faith in the sacrifice of Christ for the forgiveness of his or her sins. God the Father grants His grace to each believer upon repentance of sins and baptism by immersion, which is the outward manifestation of repentance. Through grace, the believer's sins are forgiven and the righteousness of Christ is imputed to him or her.

Grace establishes a new spiritual relationship between the believer and God the Father and Jesus Christ. Through the unearned and unmerited gift of grace, the believer is not only chosen, called, forgiven, and accepted by the Father through His Beloved, but is also begotten with the Holy Spirit, making him or her a child of God and an heir of eternal life. From this point, the spiritually begotten believer begins a new life under grace.

Importantly, grace does not grant a license to practice sin by ignoring or rejecting the commandments of God. Only those who keep God's commandments can abide in His love and remain under His grace. Every believer who receives the grace of God has a personal obligation to forsake his or her old, sinful thoughts and practices and to live a new life, growing daily in the grace and knowledge of Christ. For every believer who lives under grace, Jesus acts as Redeemer, High Priest, and Advocate. If the believer commits a sin, Jesus intercedes to propitiate the Father and to obtain His mercy and grace. The grace of God, which comes through Jesus Christ, keeps the repentant believer in a *continual* state of blamelessness.

CHAPTER TWELVE

The Ultimate Revelation of Jesus Christ— From a Speck of Dust to a Son of God

Jesus promised His apostles that He would in time reveal many things to them through the power of the Holy Spirit (John 16:12-14). Some two decades later, Jesus began to reveal new understanding to His followers—but not all at once. As we saw in the last chapter, when Paul wrote to the Galatians in 53 AD and to Romans in 57 AD, he disclosed the knowledge of the "sonship of God" (Gal. 4:5-6; Rom 8:15)—*new* knowledge concerning the destiny of those who are "called and chosen." This was the first time the phrase "sonship of God" appeared in any of the apostles' writings. Moreover, it marked the beginning of Jesus' "later revelations" to the apostles.[1]

Jesus often talked about the resurrection (Matt. 22:23-33; Luke 14:14; John 5:28-29; 11:24-25). Yet He shared few details—except to note that those in the resurrection *do not marry* nor are they *given in marriage* (Mark 12:25). However, when Paul wrote to the Corinthians in 56 AD, he wrote extensively about the resurrection from the dead, primarily because some were saying that there was no such resurrection (I Cor. 15:12-13). Apparently, many in the Corinth church still adhered to Greek philosophy and the false idea of the "immortality of the soul" rather than the resurrection of the dead.[2] As Paul notes, they were shamefully lacking in the knowledge of God (verse 34).

In defense of the resurrection, Paul declared that after Christ was raised from the dead He appeared to Peter, James, and eventually all of the apostles—and was seen by over 500 brethren at one time. Ultimately, Jesus personally appeared to Paul (verses 5-8). In his epistle, once Paul had reestablished the *fact* of Jesus' resurrection, he showed that if there is no resurrection from the dead, then Christ Himself was not raised: "For if there is no resurrection from *the* dead, neither has Christ been raised. And if Christ has not been raised, then our preaching *is* in vain, and your faith *is* also in vain. And we are also found *to be* false witnesses of God; because we have testified of God that He raised Christ, Whom He did not raise, if indeed *the* dead are not raised. For if *the* dead are not raised, neither has Christ been raised. But if Christ has not been raised, your faith *is* vain; you are still in your sins, and those who have fallen asleep in Christ have then perished" (I Cor. 15:13-18).

For Paul, Jesus' resurrection was proof of the promise of the resurrection of the saints. He adds, "But now Christ has been raised from *the* dead; He has become the Firstfruit of those who have fallen asleep. For since by man *came* death, by Man also *came the* resurrection of *the* dead. For as in Adam all die, so also in Christ shall all be made alive. But each in his own order: Christ *the* Firstfruit; then, those who are Christ's at His coming" (verses 20-23).

Paul continues to write in great detail about the resurrection of the dead. Undoubtedly, the *new* knowledge he brings out was part of the "later revelation" promised by Jesus: "Nevertheless, someone will say, '**How are the dead raised? And with what body do they come?**' Fool! What you sow does not come to life unless it dies.

"And what you sow *is* not the body that shall be; rather, *it is* bare grain—it may be of wheat, or one of the other *grains*; and God gives it a body according to His will, and to each of the seeds its own body. *Likewise*, not all flesh *is* the same flesh. Rather, *there is* one flesh of men, and another flesh of beasts, and another of fish, and another of birds.

"And *there are* heavenly bodies, and earthly bodies; but the glory of the heavenly *is* different, and the *glory* of the earthly *is* different. *There is* one glory of *the* sun, and another glory of *the* moon, and another glory of *the* stars; for *one* star differs from *another* star in glory. **So also *is* the resurrection of the dead**.

"**It is sown in corruption; it is raised in incorruption. It is sown in dishonor; it is raised in glory. It is sown in weakness; it is raised in power. It is sown a natural body; it is raised a spiritual body. There is a natural body, and there is a spiritual body**; accordingly, it is written, 'The first man, Adam, became a living soul; the last Adam *became* an ever-living Spirit.'

"However, **the spiritual *was* not first, but the natural—then the spiritual**. The first man *is* of the earth—made of dust. The second Man *is* the Lord from heaven. As *is* the one made of dust, so also *are all* those who are made of dust; and as *is* the heavenly *one*, so also *are all* those who are heavenly. **And as we have borne the image of the *one* made of dust, we shall also bear the image of the heavenly *One***" (verses 35-49).

As Paul demonstrates, the resurrection of those who are Christ's will take place *at His return*. Only at that time will they become immortal spirit beings: "Now this I say, brethren, that flesh and blood cannot inherit *the* kingdom of God, nor does corruption inherit incorruption. Behold, **I show you a mystery: we shall not all fall asleep, but we shall all be changed**, in an instant, in *the* twinkling of an eye, at the last trumpet; for *the* trumpet shall sound, and **the dead shall be raised incorruptible, and we shall be**

changed. **For this corruptible must put on incorruptibility, and this mortal must put on immortality** [which only comes from God]. Now when this corruptible shall have put on incorruptibility, and this mortal shall have put on immortality, **then shall come to pass the saying that is written: 'Death is swallowed up in victory' "** (verses 50-54; also see I Thess. 4:15-17).

Vital Hidden Knowledge

While in prison in Rome (about 61 to 63 AD), Paul wrote epistles to the Ephesians, Philippians, and Colossians. These epistles contain key aspects of Jesus' "later revelations." In Colossians, Paul writes that some of this revealed knowledge had actually been *hidden* "from ages and generations." In fact, this knowledge was so important that it would actually serve to *complete* the Word of God—to fill it to the full!

Notice: "Now, I am rejoicing in my sufferings for you, and I am filling up in my flesh that which is behind of the tribulations of Christ, for the sake of His body, which is the church; of which I became a servant, according to the administration of God that *was* **given** *to* **me for you** *in order* **to complete the Word of God;** *even* **the mystery that has been hidden from ages and from generations, but has now been revealed to His saints; to whom God did will to make known what** *are* **the riches of the glory of this mystery** among the Gentiles; **which is <u>Christ in you, the hope of glory</u>** " (Col. 1:24-27).

Paul shows here that the spiritual *work of God* in each believer centers on the spiritual reality of "Christ in you." Indeed, it is by the inner workings of the Holy Spirit in your mind and heart that you grow in grace and knowledge. This is precisely how God is developing within you the very character of Jesus. Paul elsewhere describes this process as Christ being "formed in you" (Gal. 4:19). This is *real* transformation—or conversion—the renewing of your mind by the power of God (Rom. 12:2). To accomplish this, you are to yield yourself to God in love and obedience. Paul admonished: "Let this mind be in you, which *was* also in Christ Jesus" (Phil. 2:5).

In Ephesians, perhaps the most spiritual and inspiring of Paul's epistles, the apostle declares that this revelation was not only given to him, but also to *all* the apostles and prophets: "For this cause I, Paul, *am* the prisoner of Christ Jesus for you Gentiles, if indeed you have heard of the ministry of the grace of God that was given to me for you; how **He made known to me by revelation the mystery** (even as I wrote briefly before, so that when you read *this*, you will be able to comprehend **my understanding in the mystery of Christ), which in other generations was not made known to the**

**sons of men, as it <u>has now been revealed to His holy apostles and proph-
ets by *the* Spirit</u>**; that the Gentiles might be joint heirs, and a joint body,
and joint partakers of His promise in Christ through the gospel, of which I
became a servant according to the gift of the grace of God, *which was* given
to me through the inner working of His power.

"To me, who am less than the least of all the saints, was this grace given,
that I might preach the gospel among the Gentiles—*even* the unsearchable
riches of Christ; and that I might enlighten all *as to* what *is* **the fellowship
of the mystery that has been hidden from the ages in God**, Who created
all things by Jesus Christ" (Eph. 3:1-9). As we will see, this profound mystery of God—never before made known until Paul's time—has its begin-
nings in the ancient world.

Planned Before the Foundation of the World

While God's *mystery* concerning His magnificent purpose and plan for
the "called and chosen and faithful" remained hidden until the first century
AD, it was *planned* from the beginning. However, it could only be revealed
after Jesus the Messiah, the Creator and Savior of mankind, had completed
His ministry, died for the sins of the world, and been raised to life.

In fact, the apostle John writes that Jesus' death for the sins of mankind
was *planned* from the foundation of the world: "[T]he Lamb slain from *the*
foundation of *the* world" (Rev. 13:8). This verifies that Jesus had to die for
the sins of the world before the complete knowledge of God's plan could be
revealed.

As we have seen, after His resurrection Jesus began to reveal basic things
about God's plan to His apostles, opening their minds to the Scriptures
(Luke 24:44-45). (Little did they know at that time that they would actually
have a part in completing the Word God.) When the proper time came, Jesus
began to reveal additional truths to them, beginning with the "sonship of
God." Paul writes that *before* the foundation of the world God actually
planned and predetermined this sonship status for those "called, chosen, and
faithful." Notice:

"Paul, an apostle of Jesus Christ by *the* will of God, to the saints who are
in Ephesus and to *the* faithful in Christ Jesus: Grace and peace *be* to you
from God our Father and *the* Lord Jesus Christ. Blessed *be* the God and
Father of our Lord Jesus Christ, Who has blessed us with every spiritual
blessing in the heavenly *things* with Christ; **according as He has personally chosen us** [all who receive the sonship of God] for Himself [in His plan
that was conceived] **before *the* foundation of *the* world** in order that we
might be holy and blameless before Him in love; <u>**having predestinated us**</u>

for sonship to Himself through Jesus Christ, according to the good **pleasure of His own will,** to *the* praise of *the* glory of His grace, wherein He has made us objects of *His* grace in the Beloved *Son*; in Whom we have redemption through His blood, *even* the remission of sins, according to the riches of His grace, which He has made to abound toward us in all wisdom and intelligence; **having made known to us the mystery of His own will, according to His good pleasure, which He purposed in Himself**.

"That in *the divine* plan for the fulfilling of *the* times, He might bring all things together in Christ, both the things in the heavens and the things upon the earth. *Yes,* in Him, in Whom **we also have obtained an inheritance, having been predestinated according to His purpose, Who is working out all things according to the counsel of His own will**; that we might be to *the* praise of His glory, who first trusted in the Christ" (Eph. 1:1-12).

The Mystery of God Revealed

The apostle Peter also received this amazing revelation of God's plan for the saints. So overwhelming is this knowledge that Peter describes it in the most exalted terms: "Simon Peter, a servant and an apostle of Jesus Christ, to those who have obtained *the* same precious faith as ours by *the* righteousness of our God and Savior, Jesus Christ: Grace and peace be multiplied to you in *the* knowledge of God and of Jesus our Lord, according as His divine power has given to us all things that *pertain* to life and godliness, through the knowledge of Him Who called us by *His own* glory and virtue; through which **He has given to us the greatest and *most* precious promises, that through these you may become partakers of *the* divine nature,**[3] having escaped the corruption *that is* in *the* world through lust" (II Peter 1:1-4).

Think of it! Those who are "called, chosen, and faithful" will receive the "divine nature"—the very nature of God! *That is the wonderful mystery of God!* What an awesome promise God has given to those who love Him—to those who are called according to His eternal purpose—the *full, literal, spiritual* **sonship of God!**

Because of the magnitude of this promise, Peter exhorts the brethren to apply themselves with all diligence to develop the godly character that is fitting to receive the divine nature: "And for this very reason also, having applied all diligence besides, add to your faith, virtue; and to virtue, knowledge; and to knowledge, self-control; and to self-control, endurance; and to endurance, godliness; and to godliness, brotherly love; and to brotherly love, the love *of God*.

"**For *if* these things exist and abound in you, they *will* cause *you to be* neither lacking effort nor lacking fruit in the knowledge of our Lord**

Jesus Christ. But the one in whom these things are not present is *spiritually* blind—so short-sighted *that* he has forgotten that he was purified from his old sins.

"**For this reason, brethren, be even more diligent to make your calling and election sure; because *if* you are doing these things, you will never fall at any time. For in this way, you will be richly granted an entrance into the eternal kingdom of our Lord and Savior, Jesus Christ**" (verses 5-11).

The Family of God

In his epistle to the Ephesians, Paul also describes this exalted revelation of the mystery of God. He declares that it is the Father's eternal purpose to create, through the process of sonship, His *own* personal family of spirit beings—the children of God—from those "called, chosen, and faithful."

May you grasp the inspiration of Paul's words: "And that I might enlighten all *as to* what *is* the **fellowship of the mystery** that has been hidden from the ages in God, Who created all things by Jesus Christ; so that the manifold wisdom of God might now be made known through the church to the principalities and the powers in the heavenly *places*, **according to *His* eternal purpose, which He has wrought in Christ Jesus our Lord**, in Whom we have boldness and *direct* access with confidence through His *very* own faith. So then, I beseech *you* not to faint at my tribulations for you, which are *working for* your glory.

"For this cause I bow my knees to the Father of our Lord Jesus Christ, **of Whom the whole family in heaven and earth is named**, that He may grant you, according to the riches of His glory, to be strengthened with power by His Spirit in the inner man; that Christ may dwell in your hearts by faith.

"***And* that being rooted and grounded in love, you may be fully able to comprehend with all the saints what *is* the breadth and length and depth and height, and to know the love of Christ, which surpasses *human* knowledge; <u>so that you may be filled with all the fullness of God</u>!**

"Now to Him Who is able [has the power] to do exceeding abundantly above all that we ask or think, according to the power that is working in us, to Him *be* glory in the church by Christ Jesus throughout all generations, *even* into the ages of eternity. Amen" (Eph. 3:9-21).

Paul's phrase "*filled with all the fullness of God*" is his way of echoing Peter, that we are literally to partake of the *divine nature* of God!

Chapter Twelve

The Divine Children of God the Father

In the account of the creation of Adam and Eve, God gave several important clues about His ultimate purpose for mankind: "And God said, '**Let Us make man in Our image, after Our likeness**.... **And God created man in His** *own* **image, in the image of God He created him**. He created them male and female" (Gen. 1:26-27).[3]

Unfortunately, God does not reveal here *what He meant* by man being made in the *image* and *likeness* of God. If only God had been more explicit and added "**after Our kind**"—then it would have been apparent that man was made after the *God-kind*. Moreover, there is no place in the Old Testament that clearly identifies who the "**US**" actually are. The answer to that question would come some 4,000 years later—revealed by Christ. As we will see, in His final prayer before being arrested, Jesus stated exactly who the "**US**" are—Himself and God the Father!

With the understanding we have already established, examining Jesus' final prayer will prove quite insightful. In fact, we will see that **God's ultimate purpose for the "called, chosen and, faithful," through the sonship of God, is that they are to <u>become spirit beings as literal sons and daughters of God the Father</u> in His eternal Family**. Let us carefully weigh every word of Jesus' final prayer:

"Jesus spoke these words, and lifted up His eyes to heaven and said, 'Father, the hour has come; glorify Your own Son, so that Your Son may also glorify You; since You have given Him authority over all flesh, in order that **He may give eternal life to all whom You have given Him**. For this is eternal life, that they may know You, the only true God, and Jesus Christ, Whom You did send. I have glorified You on the earth. I have finished the work that You gave Me to do.

" 'And now, **Father, glorify Me with Your own self, with the glory that I had with You before the world existed** [this is absolute proof that Jesus was the Lord God of the Old Testament before He became the Christ of the New Testament]. I have manifested Your name to the men whom You have given Me out of the world. They were Yours, and You have given them to Me, and they have kept Your Word.

" 'Now they have known that all things that You have given Me are from You. For I have given them the words that You gave to Me; and they have received *them* and truly have known that I came from You; and they have believed that You did send Me. **I am praying for them; I am not praying for the world, but for those whom You have given Me, for they are Yours**. All Mine are Yours, and all Yours *are* Mine; and I have been glorified in them.

" 'And I am no longer in the world, but these are in the world, and I am coming to You. **Holy Father, keep them in Your name, those whom You have given Me, <u>so that they may be one, even as We</u> *are one*** [that means after the God-kind, in the Family of God].

" 'When I was with them in the world, I kept them in Your name. I protected those whom You have given Me, and not one of them has perished except the son of perdition, in order that the Scriptures might be fulfilled. But now I am coming to You; and these things I am speaking *while yet* in the world, that they may have My joy fulfilled in them. I have given them Your words, and the world has hated them because they are not of the world, just as I am not of the world. I do not pray that You would take them out of the world, but that You would **keep them from the evil one**. They are not of the world, just as I am not of the world.

" '**Sanctify them** [that is, make them holy] **in Your truth; Your Word is the truth** [the words of God are "spirit and life" (John 6:63)]. Even as You did send Me into the world, I also have sent them into the world. **And for their sakes I sanctify Myself, so that they also may be sanctified in *Your* truth**.

" 'I do not pray for these only, but also for those who shall believe in Me through their word; **that <u>they all may be one</u>, even as You, Father, *are* in Me, and I in You; that <u>they also may be one in US</u>** [in the Family of God the Father and Jesus Christ].... And I have given them the glory that You gave *to* Me, **in order <u>that they may be one, in the same way *that* We are one: I in them, and You in Me, that they may be perfected</u>** [through the process of the sonship of God] **into one; and that the world may know that You did send Me, and have loved them as You have loved Me**.

" 'Father, I desire that those whom You have given Me may also be with Me where I am, so that they may behold My glory, which You have given Me; because You did love Me before *the* foundation of *the* world. Righteous Father, the world has not known You; but I have known You, and these have known that You did send Me. And I have made known Your name to them, and will make *it* known; **so that the love with which You have loved Me may be in them, and I in them**' " (John 17:1-26).

In Jesus' final prayer, He requested *four times* that His disciples "**may be one**"—just as the Father is *in* Jesus and as Jesus is *in* the Father. We are to be perfected! Down through the generation of saints, Jesus' petitions to the Father for the *oneness* of the "called and chosen" have all been answered—and will continue to be answered until the *ultimate fulfillment* of the sonship of God at the first resurrection when Christ returns.

Indeed, the ultimate revelation that Jesus gave to His Church is this: God created mankind in His image and in His likeness so that those who receive the spiritual seed of begettal—from God the Father through the power of the Holy Spirit—will become His literal children—*after the God-kind!*

John writes: "**Behold! What *glorious* love the Father has given to us, that we should be called <u>the children of God!</u>**" (I John 3:1). The Greek word for "children" is *tekna*, which means literal children *by begettal and birth*. It is not an adoption or a case of having a "foster" father. Rather, **God the Father is our *actual* Father**!

John continues: "<u>**Beloved, now we are the children of God**</u>, and it has not yet been revealed what we shall be; but we know that when He is manifested, <u>**we shall be like Him, because we shall see Him exactly as He is**</u>" (verse 2).

At the resurrection, we will see Jesus exactly as He is! What does He look like in His full glory? In the "vision of transfiguration"—which took place just before Jesus and the disciples began their journey to Jerusalem for the Feast of Tabernacles in the fall of 29 AD—Jesus displayed His glory to Peter, James, and John (the three who would be the leading apostles). Here is what they saw: "And He was transfigured before them; and **His face shined as the sun, and His garments became white as the light**" (Matt. 17:2). In reality, Jesus was not suddenly glorified; rather, this was a *vision*, a spiritual manifestation—and it was so important that He instructed them not to tell anyone about it until He had risen from the dead.

Sixty-eight years later John was given the vision that he would record as the book of Revelation. The very first thing revealed was Jesus in His full glory: "I was in *the* Spirit on the day of the Lord; and I heard a loud voice like a trumpet behind me, saying, 'I am the Alpha and the Omega, the First and the Last'; and, 'What you see, write in a book, and send *it* to the churches that *are* in Asia: to Ephesus, and to Smyrna, and to Pergamos, and to Thyatira, and to Sardis, and to Philadelphia, and to Laodicea.'

"And I turned to see the voice that spoke with me; and when I turned, I saw seven golden lampstands; and in *the* midst of the seven lampstands ***One* like *the* Son of man, clothed in *a garment* reaching to the feet, and girded about the chest with a golden breastplate. And His head and hair *were* like white wool, white as snow; and His eyes *were* like a flame of fire; and His feet *were* like fine brass, as if *they* glowed in a furnace; and His voice *was* like *the* sound of many waters. And in His right hand He had seven stars, and a sharp two-edged sword went out of His mouth, and His countenance *was* as the sun shining in its *full* power**" (Rev. 1:10-16).

This fantastic vision of Jesus Christ was so glorious and magnificent, so awesome and overwhelming, that John fell down as dead at His feet! "And when I saw Him, I fell at His feet as if dead; but He laid His right hand upon me, saying to me, '**Do not be afraid; I am the First and the Last, even the One Who is living; for I was dead, and behold, I am alive into the ages of eternity**. Amen. And I have the keys of *the* grave and of death' " (verses 17-18). It is hard for our minds to grasp that when the "called, chosen, and faithful" are raised from the dead as spirit beings, the literal children of God the Father, we will actually see Jesus as He is!

This "later revelation" by Jesus to His apostles is truly wonderful—beyond human imagination! When all of these passages are put together, they reveal that God the Father is developing *His Family* of spirit beings **who will be His own sons and daughters—created after the God-kind!**

Notice this all-important progression: *begettal—growth—birth*. When we are baptized and received the Holy Spirit, we are *begotten* by God the Father. Presently, we strive to *grow* and *mature* spiritually. Ultimately, at the resurrection, **we will be spiritually BORN AGAIN** [4]**—born *into* the Family of God! We will be His actual children—possessing full sonship!**

The truth of the "mystery of God" is this: **All of those in the first resurrection will be changed. They will have bodies and minds composed of spirit and will have immortality. They will be the children of God the Father and will be like Him and Jesus Christ—after the God-kind.** Not only will we see Jesus as He is, we will also see God the Father face to face!

Furthermore, it is Jesus Himself who will "transform our vile bodies, that they may be **conformed to His glorious body**, according to the inner working of His own power, *whereby He is able* to subdue all things to Himself" (Phil. 3:21).

What kind of glory will we have? A glory that is comparable to the *stars of heaven*. Indeed, God promised Abraham that his spiritual seed would shine like the stars of heaven: " 'By Myself have I sworn,' says the LORD, 'because you have done this thing, and have not withheld your son, your only son; that **in blessing I will bless you, and in multiplying I will multiply your seed like the stars of the heavens**..." (Gen. 22:16-17).

The prophet Daniel also described the glory of the first resurrection: "And at that time your people shall be delivered—every one who shall be found written in the book. And many of those who sleep in the dust of the earth shall awake, some to everlasting life.... **And they who are wise shall shine as the brightness of the firmament, and they who turn many to righteousness shall shine as the stars forever and ever**" (Daniel 12:1-3). Jesus confirmed this when He said concerning the resurrection: "Then shall **the righteous shine forth as the sun** in the kingdom of their Father" (Matt. 13:43).

At the first resurrection, the saints will be taken to a gigantic Sea of Glass (Rev. 15:2) where they will receive their rewards and new names. The marriage of the Lamb and the Bride will then take place, along with the marriage supper. Finally, all the saints, now spirit beings, will descend to the earth with Jesus to finish the climatic war against the armies of the world. An angel will capture the Beast and False Prophet, casting them into the lake of fire (Rev. 19). Ultimately, Satan will be cast into the abyss and bound for a thousand years (Rev. 20:1-2).

At that time, Christ will set up the Kingdom of God with all the saints participating in bringing salvation to the people of the world: "And I saw thrones; and they that sat upon them, and judgment was given to them; and *I saw* the souls of those who had been beheaded for the testimony of Jesus, and for the Word of God, and those who did not worship the beast, or his image, and did not receive the mark in their foreheads or in their hands; and **they lived and reigned with Christ a thousand years…. This *is* the first resurrection. Blessed and holy is the one who has part in the first resurrection; over these the second death has no power. But they shall be priests of God and of Christ, and shall reign with Him a thousand years**" (Rev. 20:4-6).[5]

John's final glimpse into the Kingdom of God depicts a *new heaven* and a *new earth* prepared by God for His spiritual sons and daughters—now existing eternally in the Family of God: "Then I saw a new heaven and a new earth; for the first heaven and the first earth were passed away, and there was no more sea. And I, John, saw the holy city, *the* new Jerusalem, coming down from God out of heaven, prepared as a bride adorned for her husband.

"And I heard a great voice from heaven say, 'Behold, the tabernacle of God *is* with men [and women, now made spiritually perfect]; and **He shall dwell with them, and they shall be His people; and God Himself shall be with them *and be* their God**. And God shall wipe away every tear from their eyes; and *there* shall not be any more death, or sorrow, or crying; neither shall *there* be any more pain, because the former things have passed away.'

"And He Who sits on the throne said, 'Behold, I make all things new.' Then He said to me, 'Write, for these words are true and faithful.' And He said to me, 'It is done. I am Alpha and Omega, the Beginning and the End. To the one who thirsts, I will give freely of the fountain of the water of life. **The one who overcomes shall inherit all things; and <u>I will be his God, and he shall be My son</u>…. Blessed *are* those who keep His commandments, that they may have the right to *eat of* the tree of life, and may enter by the gates into the city**' " (Rev. 21:1-7; 22:14).

From the New Jerusalem on the new earth, the saints will reign eternally with Jesus Christ even unto the vast reaches of the universe: "Then he showed me [John] a pure river of *the* water of life, clear as crystal, flowing out from the throne of God and of the Lamb. *And* in the middle of *the* street, and on this side and that side of the river, *was the* tree of life, producing twelve *manner of* fruits, each month yielding its fruit; and the leaves of the tree *are* for *the* healing of the nations.

"And there shall be no more curse; and the throne of God and of the Lamb shall be in it; and **His servants shall serve Him, and <u>they shall see His face</u>; and His name** *is* **in their foreheads**. And there shall be no night there; for they have no need of a lamp or *the* light of *the* sun, because *the* Lord God enlightens them; **and they shall reign into the ages of eternity**" (Rev. 22:1-5).

This is why you were born—to be transformed
from a speck of dust to a Son of God!

Chapter 12 Notes:

1. Jesus also revealed numerous prophecies concerning the future. For example, the book of Revelation, written by the apostle John in 96-98 AD, contains prophecies revealed by Jesus pertaining to 1) the first century church (and beyond); 2) the end of the age, including Christ's return and establishment of the Kingdom of God; 3) post-millennial events; and 4) the period known as the "judgment" and the establishment of the new heavens and the new earth. However, for the purposes of this book, we will focus on revelations relating directly to the question, *Why were you born?*

2. For hundreds of years, Orthodox "Christianity" has believed in the pagan idea of the *immortality* of the soul. While they make a few references to the resurrection of the dead, they teach that when a person dies, his or her soul goes immediately to heaven, hell, or purgatory. There is no such teaching in the entirety of the Bible. Throughout Scripture, life beyond the grave is always associated with a resurrection from the dead.

3. *Other clues from the Old and New Testaments:* In the Old Testament there are numerous clues concerning what Jesus would later reveal to the apostles. However, these clues must be used in harmony with the New Testament in order to get a complete picture. Some of these clues are easy to understand, some are not. God tells us that He has a plan, but the details are scattered throughout the Bible and must be "searched out." Below are a few key "unexplained" clues from the Old Testament concerning God's plan and the ultimate glory promised to those who are "called, chosen, and faithful":

A) In Isaiah, God proclaims that He has *planned everything* from the beginning: "Who has planned and done *it*, **calling forth the generations from the beginning?** I, the LORD, *am* the first and the last; I *am* He" (Isa. 41:4). This confirms that God *has* a plan—reaching all the way back to "the beginning." But, again, the details are scattered throughout the Bible.

B) " 'I am the Alpha and the Omega, *the* Beginning and *the* Ending,' says the Lord, 'Who is, and Who was, and Who *is* to come—the Almighty.'... 'I am the Alpha and the Omega, the First and the Last' " (Rev. 1:8, 11).

C) "Thus says the LORD, the Holy One of Israel, and the One who formed him, 'Ask Me of **things that are to come concerning My sons**, and concerning the work of My hands' " (Isa. 45:11).

D) Under God's inspiration, King David declares of mankind, "**For You have made him a little lower than God and have crowned him**

with glory and honor" (Psa. 8:5). Yet, we are not given the reason for this incredible statement!

E) David proclaims, "As for me, I will **behold Your face** in righteousness; I shall be satisfied, **when I awake, with Your likeness**" (Psa. 17:15). Moses was told He could not look on the face of God. So what is David referring to? Also, since man is already made in the *likeness* of God, what does it mean to "awaken with God's likeness"?

F) Again, David declares, "God stands in the congregation of the mighty; He judges among **the gods**.... I have said, '**You are gods** [Hebrew *elohim*; gods]; **and all of you are sons of the Most High**' " (Psa. 82:1, 6).

G). In John 10, Jesus quotes Psalm 82 to give biblical authority to His claim of being the Son of God: "Jesus answered them, 'Is it not written in your law, "I said, '**You are gods**' "? **If He called them gods** [Greek *theoi*; gods] to whom the Word of God came (and the Scriptures cannot be broken), *why* do you say *of Him* Whom the Father has sanctified and sent into the world, "You are blaspheming," because I said, "I am *the* Son of God" '? " (verses 34-36).

4. For an explanation concerning being *born again*, please see Appendix 6.

5. After the 1,000-year reign of Christ and the saints, Satan is loosed for a short season to test the nations (Rev. 20:7-10); afterwards is the second resurrection and "Great White Throne Judgment" period where salvation is made available to the billions who have never been called (verses 11-15); then comes the new heaven and new earth (and the New Jerusalem) with God the Father coming to the earth to dwell with men made perfect for eternity (Rev. 21:1-6). See Appendix 3, *What Happens After Death?*

Eternal Glory

Blessed *be* the God and Father of our Lord Jesus Christ,
Who has blessed us with every spiritual blessing
in the heavenly *things* with Christ ....

That the God of our Lord Jesus Christ, the Father of glory,
may give you *the* spirit of wisdom and revelation
in *the* knowledge of Him.
And may the eyes of your mind be enlightened
in order that you may comprehend what is the
hope of His calling, and what *are* the riches of the glory of
His inheritance in the saints ....

For I reckon that the sufferings
of the present time *are* not worthy *to be compared*
with the glory that shall be revealed in us ....

And they who are wise shall shine as the brightness
of the firmament, and they who turn many to righteousness
shall shine as the stars forever and ever ....
Then shall the righteous shine forth as the sun
in the kingdom of their Father ....

And I shall be a Father to you, and you shall be
My sons and daughters, says *the* Lord Almighty ....

O *the* depth of *the* riches of both *the* wisdom
and *the* knowledge of God!
How unfathomable *are* His judgments
and unsearchable *are* His ways! ....
For from Him, and through Him, and unto Him *are* all things;
to Him *be* the glory into the ages of eternity. Amen.

Eph. 1:3, 17-18; II Cor. 6:18; Rom. 8:18;
Dan. 12:3; Matt. 13:43; Rom. 11:33, 36

The Glory of the Stars of Heaven

"The heavens declare the glory of God, and the firmament proclaims His handiwork" (Psa. 19:1). God promised Abraham that his "spiritual seed" would be like "the stars of heaven" (Gen. 22:17). By declaring this to Abraham, God was symbolically revealing that the *spiritual children of God*, the "spiritual seed," would receive magnificent glory comparable to the stars of heaven. Paul confirms that those in the first resurrection will receive glory, symbolically compared to the glory of the stars of heaven: "*There is* one glory of *the* sun, and another glory of *the* moon, and another glory of *the* stars; for *one* star differs from *another* star in glory. So also *is* the resurrection of the dead. It is sown in corruption; it is raised in incorruption. It is sown in dishonor; it is raised in glory" (I Cor. 15:41-43). The following pictures of the heavenly stars are presented to give us a symbolic glimpse of the coming glory that God will give to the "called, chosen and faithful"—the spirit sons and daughters of God the Father.

Butterfly Nebula

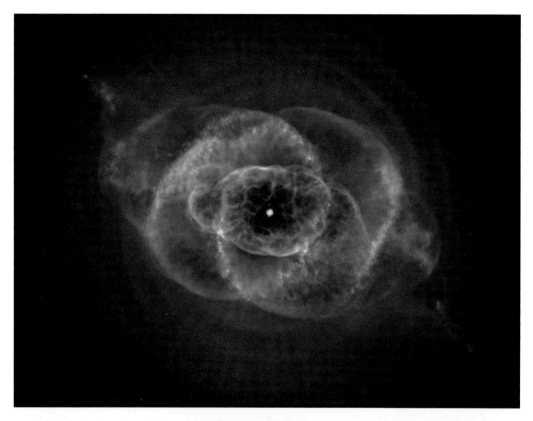

Catseye Nebula

Star Cluster Westerlund 2

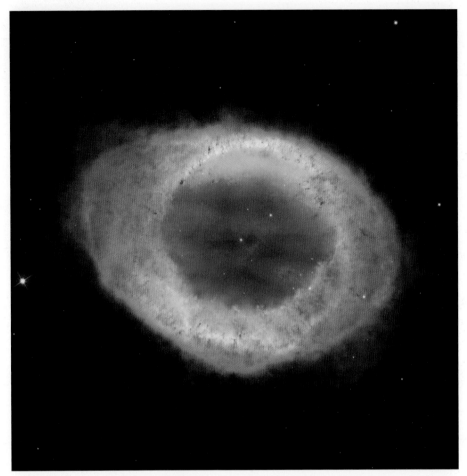

Helix Nebula Eye of God

Interacting Galaxies NGC 2207 and IC 2163

Milky Way Galaxy

NGC 3603

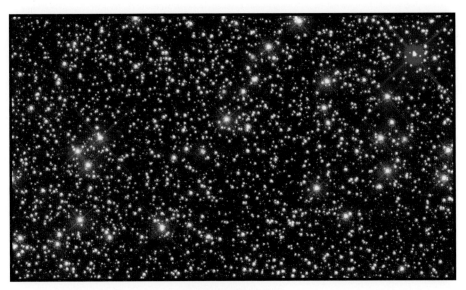

Omega Centuari

Pillars and Jets in Carina

Rosetta Nebula

Sombrero Galaxy

eXtreme Deep field

Supernova Remnant Cassiopeia A

The Antennae

Pillars of Creation

Galaxy 1080p

CONCLUSION

This book has unveiled for you the answer to the ultimate question—*Why were you born?* You have read the inspired passages from the Word of God that unlock the "mystery of God, hidden from ages and generations." It is the author's heartfelt desire that this knowledge will magnify your understanding of the awe-inspiring love that God the Father and Jesus Christ have for you—that you will come to deeply comprehend the true meaning of the "sonship of God" so that *you too* may become one of the "called, chosen, and faithful," so that *you* may become an eternal son or daughter of God the Father, made after the God-kind!

Indeed, *one final question* remains: Now that you have this vital knowledge of God's marvelous plan, what will you choose to do? Will you *act* on this wonderful knowledge and respond to God's call?

God says that "If you seek Him, He will be found by you" (II Chron. 15:2). The prophet Isaiah says that *now* is the time to seek God: "**Seek the LORD while He may be found; call upon Him while He is near**. Let the wicked forsake his way, and the unrighteous man his thoughts; and **let him return to the LORD, and He will have mercy upon him; and to our God, for He will abundantly pardon**. 'For My thoughts *are* not your thoughts, nor your ways My ways,' says the LORD. 'For *as* the heavens are higher than the earth, so are My ways higher than your ways, and My thoughts than your thoughts' " (Isa. 55:6-9).

Likewise, Jesus promises us this: "Ask, and it shall be given to you. Seek, and you shall find. Knock, and it shall be opened to you. For everyone who asks receives, and the one who seeks finds, and to the one who knocks it shall be opened" (Matt. 7:7-8).

You may be wondering, *Where do I begin?* You begin by going directly to God the Father in prayer—on your knees—confessing your sins and acknowledging that you have lived contrary to His way of life as outlined by His laws and commandments (I John 1:6-10; 2:1-2). As you yield your heart and mind to God, as you seek Him and begin to obey His will in your life, He will graciously lead you to real repentance (Rom. 2:4).

Upon deep, godly repentance, God will forgive your sins by His grace and mercy through the sacrifice and shed blood of Christ (Rom. 3:23-31). Then you must be baptized by full immersion in water—by which you enter into the New Covenant and receive the begettal of the Holy Spirit of God the Father. This is the beginning of your sonship of God!

When you are raised out of that "watery grave," you are to walk in newness of life. You are to *live by every word of God* in loving obedience to your heavenly Father—as led by the power of the Holy Spirit.

Conclusion

As you grow in grace and knowledge, you will hunger and thirst after the righteousness of God. You will experience a deep desire to love God with all your heart, with all your mind, and with all your strength. With God the Father and Jesus dwelling in your heart and mind through the power of the Holy Spirit, you will begin to develop the "mind of Christ."

You will begin to grasp the *full meaning* of the often quoted verse: "For God so loved the world that He gave His only begotten Son, so that everyone who believes in Him may not perish, but may have everlasting life" (John 3:16). Here, the Greek for "believes" means so much more than the mere acknowledgement of Jesus' role as Savior. Rather, the present tense participle *pisteuon* describes one who "continually believes" in Jesus—that is, belief that is expressed by a deep, ongoing conviction of faith manifested in loving obedience to God.

Indeed, salvation is a life-long process of growth and overcoming. But as God has promised, He *will* fulfill His plan and purpose for you: "According as His divine power has given to us all things that *pertain* to life and godliness, through the knowledge of Him Who called us by *His own* glory and virtue; through which **He has given to us the greatest and *most* precious promises, that through these you may become partakers of *the* divine nature…**" (II Pet. 1:3-4).

Ultimately, when Jesus returns, you will be granted entrance into the immortal, divine Family of God—created after the God-kind, possessing God's own divine nature!

So awesome and wonderful is God's plan that the apostle Paul wrote this prayer of encouragement *for you* and for all of those faithful in Christ:

"That the God of our Lord Jesus Christ, the Father of glory, may give you *the* spirit of wisdom and revelation in *the* knowledge of Him. *And* may the eyes of your mind be enlightened in order that you may comprehend what is the hope of His calling, and what *are* the riches of the glory of His inheritance in the saints, and what is the exceeding greatness of His power toward us who believe, according to the inner working of His mighty power, which He wrought in Christ, when He raised Him from *the* dead, and set *Him* at His right hand in the heavenly *places*, far above every principality and authority and power and lordship, and every name that is named—not only in this age, but also in the *age* to come….

"[And] that He may grant you, according to the riches of His glory, to be strengthened with power by His Spirit in the inner man; that Christ may dwell in your hearts by faith; *and* that being rooted and grounded in love, you may be fully able to comprehend with all the saints what *is* the breadth and length and depth and height, and to know the love of Christ, which surpasses *human* knowledge; so **that you may be filled with all the fullness of God**. Now to Him Who is able to do exceeding abundantly above all that we ask or think, according to the power that is working in us, to Him *be* glory in the church by Christ Jesus throughout all generations, *even* into the ages of eternity. Amen" (Eph. 1:17-21; 3:16-21).

This is why you were born!

Epilogue

To help you begin to fulfill your destiny, the Christian Biblical Church of God has available, at no cost, many essential biblical publications, studies, and audio/video messages that will show you *how* to become one of the "called, chosen, and faithful."

***Church at Home*:** This is one of our primary Web sites, **churchathome.org**. Its focus is on basic teachings of the Bible and scriptural Christianity. With 360 half-hour video segments, this site compares the truth of God's Word to the false teachings of nominal Christianity. We cover current news and Bible prophecy, and examine the problems of this world in the light of the Scriptures.

This is the place to begin. You can search our directory and select the videos that will help you the most. For starters, we recommend: *To Return to God; What is Sin?; Which Day is the True Sabbath of God?; The Love of God Series; How to Pray Series; Why Were You Born?; The Addicted Society; Obsessed with Sex; How Old is the Earth?; How the Christian World was Deceived; The Truth About Sunday-Keeping; The Truth About the Holidays; The Truth About God's Holy Days*—and much, much more.

***Christian Biblical Church of God* Web site:** This site is simply **cbcg.org**. It is one of the largest biblical sites in the world—and is used by nearly one million truth-seekers each year!

This site contains nearly 1,500 full-length (90-minute), in-depth audio messages and over 400 video messages. Many studies cover Bible prophecy in great detail. There are also verse-by-verse studies of many of the books of the Bible. And every audio message includes transcripts.

This is a vast site—packed with information covering almost every biblical teaching and doctrine you can imagine. It is an excellent resource for messages on Christian growth. All of this is freely available so you can learn the truth of God's Word and grow in the grace and knowledge of Jesus Christ.

***A Faithful Version*:** This is our third Web site, **afaithfulversion.org**. This site is solely devoted to *The Holy Bible In Its Original Order—A Faithful Version With Commentary*. The site is easy to use. It features the entire Bible, book by book, in the original manuscript order. There is also an *audio reading* that accompanies each chapter—as well as the commentary and the 26 appendices. These appendices give detailed explanations of difficult-to-understand passages of Scripture. *The Holy Bible in Its Original Order* is one of the finest English translations in the world—and is sure to make your Bible studies come alive!

Appendix One

Seven Proofs God Exists

Christians today often find themselves surrounded by an increasingly hostile world. Atheists proclaim that there is *no* God, no Creator, and that Christians are foolish and naïve for their belief in a higher power. Agnostics say they just don't know—and that *if* God does exist, it cannot be proven. Other so-called "enlightened thinkers" allow for the existence of a God, but say that He is aloof, detached, and disinterested in man.

Is that so? As a Christian, can you prove the existence of God? And can you do so using sound reasoning and scientific principles?

The answer is *yes!* You should be able to defend your faith. Below are seven irrefutable proofs of the existence of the Creator God.* And remember, Christians should have no fear of science. The fact is, *true* science—science that is correctly understood and applied—is never at odds with the Bible. As we will see, God Himself is, in fact, the supreme scientist of the universe.

Proof One: Creation Demands a Creator

The theory of evolution provides the atheist with an "explanation" of creation without a Creator. But this misguided "rationalism" cannot account for the origin of the universe, of matter, or of life. It only *presumes* that some "random cosmic event" began a process that has somehow culminated in human life. But more and more honest scientists, biologists, geneticists, and geologists are now admitting that the "big bang" theory is utterly insufficient to account for the massive complexity we see around us. Such complexity testifies of a Maker; such incredible design testifies of a Designer. In short, *creation demands a Creator!*

Indeed, it is as David the psalmist wrote, "The heavens themselves declare the glory of God, and the sky wonderfully displays His handiwork" (Psa. 19:1; paraphrased).

It is a scientific fact that there has been no past eternity of matter. In other words, matter has not always existed. Want proof? Radioactive matter is constantly breaking down, changing into a more stable form—ultimately *lead*. If matter has always existed, all radioactive elements would have long ago decomposed into simpler forms, into lead. Thus, the presence of radioactive matter proves that matter itself has only existed a relatively short period of time.

This means there was a time when matter *came into existence*.

But how? Even *if* the "big bang" theory was true, where did the matter itself come from? Evolutionary theory hinges on the idea of *gradual* transformation. Can your mind imagine something gradually coming into existence *out of nothing?* Only a special, *instantaneous creation* can account for the sudden appearance of matter. And that demands a Creator!

Proof Two: Natural Laws Demand a Lawmaker

Proponents of evolution speak often of *natural laws*—laws assumed to be in operation at the time of the so-called "big bang." In other words, the outcome of this supposed cosmic event was *fully dependent* on certain physical laws. Today, scientists understand and utilize scores of these laws—such as the laws of gravity, of thermodynamics, of inertia and motion, of mass and velocity, of energy. These, and many others, are definite, immutable laws that direct how matter and energy interact. Indeed, our universe is *governed* by indisputable laws.

Evolutionary scientists readily admit that such laws were involved in the formation of the universe—and that the same laws are *actively involved* in how the universe maintains its status quo. Yet they cannot account for the *origin* of such laws; they are just assumed to exist.

The fact is, these active, inexorable laws of the natural universe are evidence of a Creator. Evolutionists may conveniently ignore the question of the origin of such laws, but Christians know that there is but one true *Lawgiver* (James 4:12).

Proof Three: Life Comes Only from Life

The theory of evolution teaches that life as we know it evolved from lower, simpler forms of life. But evolutionists cannot account for the *origin* of life—even simple organic forms. Life itself is incredibly complex—and there is a huge chasm separating life from non-life, dividing living matter from lifeless matter. No scientist has ever bridged that gap—nor will they ever do so! For it is a *law of nature* that life can only spring from preexisting life!

Science has never been able to take even previously living tissue—let alone simple organic matter—and impart life to it. Indeed, how could lifeless matter possibly spontaneously give rise to life? This gap between life and non-life is unfathomable, insurmountable for man—but not for God. He alone has the ability to literally *breathe life* into lifeless matter (Gen. 2:7).

This immutable *law of biogenesis*—that *life can come only from life*—is absolute proof of a Creator!

Proof Four: The Interdependency of Nature Demands a Creator

Look around you. You live in a complex, intricate world—a world characterized by design, order, harmony and *interdependency*. *Every* part of a flower has a purpose—there are no "useless" parts—and a flower's vibrant color and fragrance draws in vital pollinators. In turn, pollinating bees "know" how to make honey from plant nectar in order to survive. In nature, one form of life is highly dependent on other life forms. And nothing lives or dies to itself, as everything that dies provides some element necessary for the continuation of life itself. Human life in particular is completely dependent on plant and animal life.

This high level of interdependency found throughout nature poses serious problems for evolutionists. Without the bee, many plants could never reproduce and survive; without the plants, bees could never survive. *Which came first?*

Evolution demands gradual change based on mutation and random chance. But did bees and plants really *accidentally* evolve simultaneously—developing a complex life-and-death interdependency at "just the right time"? Or, does not their complex interdependency demand a Creator?

Proof Five: Who Is the Master Clockmaker?

Even the simplest of clocks are complex mechanical devices. Depending on the particular design, scores of moving parts must interact precisely if a timepiece is to keep proper time. Yet even the most expensive clocks do not keep *perfect* time and will invariably need to be adjusted periodically. But what *standard* is used to establish such perfect timekeeping? What "master clock" is used to ultimately update all timepieces?

The heavens!

The great "master timepiece" of the universe—as measured by skilled astronomers—is *always* on time, never off by even a *fraction* of a second! The various celestial bodies coursing through the heavens "know" their courses—having been *set* by some unseen hand ages ago. Some "master clockmaker" planned each and every star and planet, setting each into place, establishing each orbit with a precision unparalleled in timekeeping.

Or, did our universe—*the ultimate timepiece*—result from a random "big bang"? Would not such an event create just the *opposite* of what we see—would it not create *chaos* and *imprecision* in heavenly timekeeping? What are the odds that our precise heavenly clock—*which never needs to be reset or adjusted*—could result from a random "big bang"?

It would be impossible! You would have better odds taking all of the parts of even the simplest of clocks, putting them into box, and shaking that box for a thousand years—hoping that somehow those parts would assemble themselves into an accurately running clock!

Yes—an absurd idea! But no more ridiculous than believing that the great "master clock" of the universe came into existence by random chance!

The "master timepiece" of the heavens could only exist—running perfectly now for eons—if it were planned, designed, and set into motion by the Master Clockmaker! Indeed, creation *demands* a Creator—and only the *fool* says, "there is no God" (Psa. 14:1)!

Proof Six: Is Anything Superior to Man?

As vast and magnificent as the universe is, one has to admit that it is *inferior* to the mind of man. Indeed, the galaxies have no thoughts, no will; the cosmos does not create, hope or dream. Rather, they are inanimate, and thus infinitely *inferior* to the human mind. Man can know, think, reason, create, design, invent, etc. Man can explore the vastness of the seas, examine the inner workings of atoms, fly through the sky at more than the speed of sound, make trips to the moon and back, communicate instantaneously around the world via computers, the internet satellites and digital devices.

There is almost nothing that man cannot do. However, man cannot create anything that is *superior* to himself—to his own mind. Think about this. What have you designed, built or created from nothing? Is it superior to yourself? Of course not. That would be impossible—for *you* are its creator.

There is nothing in this material universe that is superior to man—and you cannot create something greater than yourself. This begs the question: Could any power, force or intelligence *inferior* to man be responsible for creating mankind? If God does not exist, if there is no Creator—then, we are forced to admit that something *inferior* to ourselves created us! But that is impossible! The only answer is that some Power or Being far greater than man—far superior to the mind of man—must have created humankind!

Proof Seven: Changed Lives and Answered Prayer

Perhaps the most profound proof of God's existence can be found in His active involvement in people's lives. Atheists and secularists scoff at this notion because *they* have never experienced the *power* that leads to a changed life, the *inspiration* that leads to wholesale transformation in a believer, the *peace* that comes from genuine reconciliation with one's Maker. Atheists don't know what it's like to pour one's heart out to the God of the universe and *know* that He hears; secular humanists can't imagine the joy that comes from the knowledge that one's eternal life is secure. What *atheist* has had his prayers answered? And what *evolutionist* has witnessed divine intervention?

Only those who truly belong to God *know* and *see* and *experience* these powerful proofs of the absolute existence of our Creator God!

* These proofs of God's existence are adapted from material produced by Ambassador College, Pasadena, Calif., 1971-72.

Appendix Two

Did God Create Satan the Devil?

To millions of people today, the devil is but a fairy-tale character—a blood-red grotesque creature with horns, a pointed tail, and dragon-like wings. As such, he is viewed as the mythical embodiment of evil. Few, however, take the idea of a *real* devil seriously.

But the Bible teaches that Satan the devil is very real, and very dangerous. But where did Satan come from? What is his purpose? Is he actively involved with humanity? Did God create him? If so, why?

Satan loves the popular view that he is but a mythical creature, because this keeps people *unaware* of the reality that he is the "god" of this present age (II Cor. 4:4). The Bible shows Satan—the name means *enemy* or *adversary*—to be a powerful spirit being with a great deal of influence over humanity. In fact, Satan is *actively* "deceiving the whole world" (Rev. 12:9).

The apostle Peter warns Christians that the devil is prowling around looking for someone to spiritually devour (I Pet. 5:8). Indeed, Satan—along with his demon cohorts—is mentioned numerous times in Scripture. To understand his origins, we must look to the beginning—even before the universe was created.

Satan the Devil—A Fallen Archangel

We know from Scripture that God must have created the angels *first*—for they all *shouted for joy* when God laid the foundations of the earth (Job 38:4-7). The earth was created as a jewel adorning the heavens—a spectacular planet that inspired awe in the angels.

But in Genesis we read that the earth was "without form and void"—with only darkness covering the planet (Gen. 1:2; *KJV*). The Hebrew words used here refer to something that is waste, *vain*, in absolute chaos. Did God create the earth is this manner? *No*—for God is "not the author of confusion" (I Cor. 14:33). The angels shouted for joy because it was a *perfect* creation.

A proper rendering helps us to understand: "And the earth **became** without form and void..." (Gen. 1:2). Thus, the earth was created *perfect*—but was later defiled, becoming a vast wasteland, void, chaotic. Indeed, in Isaiah 45:18, God declares that He did *not* create the earth *in vain* (the Hebrew word used here is one of the same words used in Genesis 1:2).

But how did this happen? If God did not create the earth as a wasteland, how did it come to be in that condition?

Scripture shows that God created *three* archangels—Gabriel, Michael, and Lucifer (see Luke 1:19; Jude 9; Dan. 10:13; 12:1; Rev. 12:7). These archangels had special positions at God's throne in heaven (see Ezek. 28:14, 16:).

Apparently, Lucifer was eventually assigned to oversee the earth, a position he later came to *resent*. Referring to the *spirit power* behind Tyrus, a wicked Phoenician king, the prophet Ezekiel writes: "You seal up the measure of perfection, full of wisdom, and perfect in beauty. You have been in Eden, the garden of God; every precious stone *was* your covering, the ruby, the topaz, and the diamond, the beryl, the onyx, and the jasper, the sapphire, the turquoise, and the emerald, and gold. The workmanship of your settings and of your sockets was prepared in you in the day that you were created" (Ezek. 28:12-13). Notice that this cannot literally refer to Tyrus, as this being was *perfect*, had been *in the Garden of Eden*, and was "created." Humans are not created, as such, but produced through procreation. What Ezekiel is doing is demonstrating the *spirit power* behind wicked Tyrus. The following verses make this clear: "You [Lucifer, not Tyrus] *were* **the anointed cherub that covers** [God's throne], and I set you so; you were upon the holy mountain of God; you have walked up and down in the midst of the stones of fire [in heaven]. You *were* perfect in your ways from the day that you were created, **until iniquity was found in you**" (verses 14-15).

This archangel not only once "covered" God's throne—just as the Temple "mercy seat," a type of God's throne in heaven, was covered by two angels' wings—he also later appeared *in* the Garden of Eden as a seducing serpent. This being was extraordinary, *perfect*, until *iniquity* was found in him; pride corrupted his wisdom, and his heart became filled with *vanity* (verse 17).

In a similar passage, the prophet Isaiah adds that Lucifer, in his vanity, said, "I will ascend *into* the heavens [from earth], **I will exalt my throne**"—this shows that Lucifer had a dominion, a responsibility, *on earth*—"above the stars [angels, Rev. 1:20] of God; I will also sit upon the mount of the congregation, in the sides of the north [the location of God's throne]. I will ascend above the heights of the clouds; I will be like the Most High" (Isa. 14:13-14). Lucifer apparently attempted to exalt himself above God—to take control of heaven. As Revelation brings out, this resulted in a *war* in heaven in which Lucifer—now called the Enemy, or Satan—and his angels (now demons) were cast out: "And there was war in heaven; Michael and his angels warred against the dragon, and the dragon and his angels warred. But they did not prevail, neither was their place found any more in heaven. And the great dragon was cast out, the ancient serpent who is called the

Devil and Satan, who is deceiving the whole world; he was cast down to the earth, and his angels were cast down with him" (Rev. 12:7-9).

Jude 6 proves that these rebellious angels had *abandoned* their original assignment on earth. "And the angels who **did not keep their own original domain, but deserted their habitation,** He [God] is holding in eternal bonds under darkness unto the judgment of *the* great day." Peter, writing of God's judgment for sin, notes that God "did not spare *the* **angels who sinned,** but, having cast *them* into Tartarus [a condition of restraint], delivered *them* into chains of darkness to be kept for *the* judgment [of the great day]" (II Pet. 2:4).

This powerful spirit entity—accompanied by a third of the angels—decided to challenge God for control of the universe! Looking again at Isaiah 14, the prophet writes, "How you are fallen from the heavens, O shining star [the meaning of Lucifer], son of the morning! *How* you are cut down to the ground, you who [then] weakened the nations!" (verse 12).

It was this great "war in heaven" that resulted in the earth becoming a vast wasteland! When Satan and his demons were cast out of heaven—*cast down to the earth*—one of two things happened that resulted in the destruction of the surface of the earth: 1) the earth was devastated by the war itself; or, 2) Satan, in his intense anger, purposely inflicted massive damage on the earth. Either way, the earth *became* "without form and void."

Lucifer had been a beautiful, immensely talented spirit being with tremendous authority and responsibility in God's angelic order. Through sin—jealousy, envy, pride, which quickly led to hatred and deceit—this powerful being turned against God. He became Satan—the Adversary of God and man. He hates God and His plan for man—and will stop at nothing to defeat God and ruin His plan for humanity.

Thus, God did not *create* the devil. He created a wonderful, perfect angel who—of his own choosing—*became* Satan the devil. He is a liar and deceiver, a slanderer and accuser—dedicated to destruction.

Satan—The "god" of this Present Age/World

Genesis 1:2 shows that the formerly perfect earth had been subjected to a great cataclysm of some kind—some event that left it "without form and void." That event was Satan's *great rebellion*. The remainder of Genesis two describes a *recreation*—a preparing of the earth to be the home for man. The surface of the moon was not restored, and its massive craters remain as evidence of that ancient cosmic battle.

Satan wasted no time in attempting to thwart God's plan—immediately going after Eve, using cunning guile to deceive her into disobeying God.

Remember, Ezekiel says Lucifer had been *in Eden*. Genesis two and three show that the only ones who were in the Garden of Eden were God, Adam and Eve and Satan the devil. This shows that Ezekiel 28 is referring to the covering cherub who became Satan the devil. (However, Satan had possessed the king of Tyre. It was the king who was destroyed, not Satan the devil.) Then when Satan came into the Garden of Eden apparently assumed the form of a cunning *serpent* in order to lie and deceive—to wreak havoc on God's plan. Revelation 12:9 says he continues to *actively deceive* the whole world! Indeed, the Bible makes it clear that all human civilizations, from Adam and Eve until Jesus' return, Satan has been and will continue to be broadly influenced by Satan. The apostle John writes that "**the whole world lies in *the power of* the wicked one**" (I John 5:19).

Satan is the "prince of the power of the air, the spirit that is now working within the children of disobedience" (Eph. 2:2). As the "god" of this present evil age (II Cor. 4:4; Gal. 1:4), Satan is the primary *cause* behind the wickedness that dominates human life—the *cause* of all the suffering and tragic circumstances that afflict so many.

But Satan is primarily the foe of God's chosen people—Israel and the Church. Thus, as Christians we struggle "against principalities *and* against powers, against the world rulers of the darkness of this age, against the spiritual *power* of wickedness in high *places*" (Eph. 6:12). Satan is especially deceitful in the area of religion, and few realize just how deeply Satan's deceptions have infiltrated even Christianity! He has the *entire world* duped as to the identity of the true God and how to rightly follow and worship Him. He even has his own ministers that look and sound like true ministers of God—but they are *counterfeits* (II Cor. 11:13-15). As God's elect, we must be diligent to "put on the whole amour of God" in order to "stand against the wiles of the devil" (Eph. 6:11). If we diligently *resist* Satan, he will flee from us! (James 4:7).

Jesus spoke of the devil as a real being, one with great power—but also one who could be *defeated*. Jesus Himself faced and defeated Satan (Matt. 4:1-11). Notice in verse nine that Satan offered Jesus a chance to rule the world under him. Such authority was Satan's to give, because God has, for now, allowed Satan to have dominion over this word, during this age.

But not for long! Jesus said "all power" in heaven and earth has now been given to Him (Matt. 28:18). Satan will be *removed* by Christ shortly after His coming (Rev. 20:1-3, 10), and rulership of this world will be given to the saints (Rev. 5:10; 20:4, 6). Meanwhile, we must fight the good fight and overcome Satan. It is difficult—but with God all things are possible (Matt. 19:26; Mark 9:23; 10:27; Luke 18:27). John writes these words of great comfort and encouragement: "I am writing to you, fathers, because you have known Him Who *is* from *the* beginning. I am writing to you, young men, because **you have overcome the wicked *one***. I am writing to you, little children, because you have known the Father. I wrote to you, fathers, because you have known Him Who *is* from *the* beginning. I wrote to you, young men, because you are strong, and **the Word of God is dwelling in you**, **and you have overcome the wicked *one***" (I John 2:13-14).

The *key* to overcoming Satan is to have the Word of God—Jesus the Messiah, as the living embodiment of God's inspired Word—*actively living in us!* Indeed, without Him, *we can do nothing* (John 15:5; Gal. 2:20).

Appendix Three

What Happens After Death?

Millions of people today—and more billions throughout history—have never had even the slightest chance for salvation. In fact, most have never even heard the *name* of Jesus Christ—the only name under heaven by which man may be saved (Acts 4:12). What happens to such people when they die? Are they, as many believe, "lost"?

Orthodox Christendom would have us believe that death is little more than the death of the body, while the still-conscious "immortal soul" goes on to an eternity of bliss in heaven, or to an eternity of torment in an ever-burning hell.

What does the Bible really teach about *death* and the state of the dead? What is the fate of the billions who have never known salvation through Christ?

Is the Soul Immortal?

Interestingly, Orthodox Christendom as a whole does not even pretend to get its beliefs from the Bible alone. Many, in fact, are of pagan origin. The "immortal soul" concept, for example, does not come from the Bible. If you believe the Bible is the Word of God and the only reliable source of knowledge about God, then the question is, "What does the Bible teach about life after death?"

Most religious leaders today continue to teach the immortality of the soul, despite the fact that the Bible teaches the exact opposite—that the human soul is *mortal*. It can and does *die* (Ezek. 18:20). God alone has immortality (I Tim. 6:15, 16).

The immortal soul idea can be traced back to ancient Babylonian mythology, which in various forms spread through the then-civilized world, eventually centering in Egypt in the third and second millennia BC. Greek mythology came mostly from Egypt, and its gods were simply the old Egyptian gods under different names. In the so-called "Golden Age" of Greek civilization, belief in various deities was overlaid gradually with a body of philosophy promoted by Socrates, Plato and Aristotle. A major part of Platonic philosophy was based on the supposed *dualistic* nature of man—the idea of an immortal soul trapped inside a material body. Thus, the "inner person" is actually an "immortal soul" that originated in the heavens and came down to be trapped inside a material, physical body. The material

151

body was deemed temporary and essentially evil. Accordingly, the hope of the "spiritual man" was that his conscious immortal soul could return to heaven at the death of the material body.

Most post-apostolic "church fathers" were brought up believing ideas such as the immortality of the soul prior to becoming "Christian." Through their highly influential writings, they eventually infused such ideas into the doctrines of the Roman Church. The Protestant Reformation—while it did help to correct some doctrinal errors—continued to promote the immortal soul heresy, which today underlies Protestant as well as Catholic doctrine.

What the Bible says about the *soul* requires some study. The Hebrew word translated "soul" is *nephesh,* defined as "a *breathing* creature, i.e., animal or (abstract) *vitality…*" (*Strong's Exhaustive Concordance of the Bible,* Hebrew Lexicon, item 5315). The various uses of *nephesh* simply refer to the *physical life* of air-breathing creatures—including human beings. Rather than being *separate from* the physical body, the soul is inextricably fused with the body.

When God created Adam, He made *him*—not just his body—"of the dust of the ground." Note that Adam did not *receive* a soul, but "*became* a living soul" (*nephesh*). The soul is what a person *is*—not something he "has." It's the *complete being*, both physical and nonphysical.

Can a soul die? In Ezekiel 18:4 we read, "The soul [*nephesh*] that sins, it [not just the body] shall die." For emphasis, the statement is repeated in verse 20. Some point to what Jesus said in Matthew 10:28—"Fear not them which kill the body, but are not able to kill the soul"—but they fail to read the rest of the passage. "But rather fear him [God] which is able to destroy both soul and body in hell [Greek *gehenna*]" (*KJV*). Notice, Christ did *not* say this *gehenna* fire burns the soul for eternity, but that it *destroys* the soul—burns it up, causing it to cease to exist. Christ made it clear that the soul is *not* immortal and has no life or consciousness apart from the body.

Confusing Soul with Spirit

Some misunderstanding of the biblical teaching on the soul may result from the fact that the Bible also teaches that man has a human spirit. The Hebrew word translated "spirit" is *ruach,* which in some places is also translated "breath."

Job 32:8 says there is a "spirit in man." Several passages in Proverbs refer to this human spirit (Prov. 15:13; 16:32; 20:27; 25:28). This inner spirit, which we all have, is not a separate or additional "being"—nor an "immortal soul" trapped inside of us. It is a non-physical dimension that God gives to each of us at conception and is what, in reality, makes us human (Isa. 42:5; Zech. 12:1).

It is the human spirit added to our brain that gives us a *conscious mind* with self-identity—through which we are able to learn complex subjects such as language, mathematics and design (I Cor. 2:11). The human spirit is the sum total of everything about us that is non-physical—our thoughts, imaginations, plans, hopes, dreams, feelings, emotions, attitudes—and makes us each who and what we are. The human spirit also provides God with what is comparable to a "recording" of all that we are—which at death returns to God (Eccl. 12:7). God can then use this "recording" to resurrect us back to physical (or spiritual) life with everything that was unique about us intact.

It is important to understand that even with the addition of the human spirit, it is the whole physical and spiritual package that makes up the person—the soul. The whole person *is* a soul—not *has* a soul. Neither the soul nor the human spirit retain any consciousness after death (Psalm 146:4).

Through conversion our human spirit is conjoined by God's Holy Spirit (Rom. 8:16). It is through the workings of God's Spirit with our human spirit in our minds that enables us to be able to understand the things of God (I Cor. 2:11). Those who have God's Holy Spirit added to their human spirit in this life become, at death, the "dead in Christ."

What *Is* Death?

The Bible is clear in its teaching on death and the state of the dead. The difference between being alive and being dead, according to Scripture, is not a matter of place or location—but a matter of being conscious or not conscious. Death is the total cessation of life, including consciousness. The only hope for the dead is through a resurrection back to conscious life. In fact, the Bible describes the death of humans as being identical to the death of animals (Eccl. 3:19, 20). Death is the same for all—whether righteous or unrighteous, faithful or unfaithful (Eccl. 9:2). In death, a person's thoughts perish—he or she *knows nothing*, has no consciousness, no awareness (Eccl. 9:5; Psa. 146:4). They are neither looking down from "heaven" nor roasting in a "hell" somewhere in the bowels of the earth. They are simply *dead*.

Do People Go to Heaven?

Many are surprised to learn that the Bible does not teach that anyone goes to heaven. On the contrary, Jesus—the very author of our Christian faith, whose words ought to carry far more weight than those of any would-be religious leader—stated emphatically, "No man has ascended up to heaven" (John 3:13). The apostle Peter adds, "David is not ascended into the heavens" (Acts 2:34)—he is simply dead.

Hebrews 9:27 tells us that it is appointed to *all to die once*. This first death (and lying dead for decades or centuries afterward) is neither a reward nor a punishment. It is simply what happens to everyone. In David's case—because he died "in the faith"—he will (in a future resurrection) receive the reward of the faithful. Like all the true saints who have died, he is simply waiting in his grave for the resurrection.

Another false teaching (also based on the "immortal soul" idea) insists that people go at death to a place called "Purgatory" where they suffer over long periods of time in order have their sins purged—after which they can go on to heaven. Obviously, there are no references to such a myth in Scripture. In fact, the idea denies the very sacrifice of Christ for the forgiveness of sin. When a person is truly converted—has repented of sin and accepted Christ as savior—his or her sins are totally and completely forgiven *at that time*. One does not have to undergo any punishment for such sins—now or after death.

The Resurrection—A Christian's Hope

Job asked the question in chapter 14, verse 14, "If a man die, shall he live again?" He gives the answer: "All the days of my appointed time [in the grave] I will wait, until my change comes. You shall call, and I will answer You; You shall have the desire for the work of Your hands." This change does *not* occur right at death. Job knew he would have to *wait in the grave* for an unknown period of time before God would raise him up to a *changed* state—from being dead to being alive.

Again, we must look to the words of Christ, not to those of human church leaders. The most quoted verse of the Bible—John 3:16—may also be one of its least understood. "For God so loved the world that He gave His only begotten son, that whosoever believes in Him should not..."—what? Not go to hell, but go to heaven?

Is that what Christ said?

This passage is not about living forever in a horrible place or living forever in a good place. Location isn't the issue. Christ said those who believe in Him "should not *perish*"—which means to cease to exist—"but have everlasting life."

In the book of Acts and throughout the epistles, Paul and the other apostles describe the Christian hope as being the *resurrection from the dead*. In reassuring Christians of this hope, Paul makes it clear in I Corinthians 15 that Jesus' resurrection is absolute proof of a future resurrection of the saints. He encourages the Thessalonians with similar words (I Thess. 4:13-18). Referring to the resurrection of the true Christian, Christ repeatedly said, "I will raise him up **at the last day**" (John 6:39, 40, 44, 54; 11:24).

When does God make His final decision whether a person lives forever or perishes? Does God make that decision at the time of a person's death? For those few who have been called to conversion and God's grace, now is their time of judgment. But for the majority, the time for their judgment has not yet come. Remember, the first death is neither reward nor punishment—for in Adam we all die (I Cor. 15:22). The vast majority of the dead are simply waiting for their resurrection, when they will have their opportunity for "judgment."

Is Today the Only Day of Salvation?

According to mainstream Christianity, if a person doesn't "get saved" now, in this life, he or she is lost forever. As sincere as this teaching may be, it is simply incorrect. The Bible does *not* teach the idea that this life is the only time in which people may have salvation!

Satan, the "god of this world" (II Cor. 4:4), currently holds most religious and civil leaders under his sway—having deceived such leaders at every turn (Rev. 12:9). The result is a world of culture and tradition in which whole populations are entrenched in false ways of life. Most people are so steeped in the ways of this world that they cannot possibly understand the truth of God—nor would they be willing to follow God's way of life even if they did understand. This is why, as Paul says in Romans 11:32, God has "concluded them all in unbelief"—but only for a time—"that He might have mercy on them all" in a future time of judgment.

Add to that the fact that the natural human mind simply lacks the capacity or even the desire to understand spiritual truth (I Cor. 2:11, 14). Only if God by His spirit "calls" a person—that is, *opens the mind* of an individual and imparts understanding of His truth—does that person come to repentance and conversion in this life (II Cor. 7:9-11; John 6:44; Rom. 2:4; Phil. 2:13).

Christ indicated to His disciples that such a calling has *not* been extended to most people in this life. They asked Him why He spoke to the masses in parables. He answered, "Because it has been **given to you** to know the mysteries of the kingdom of heaven, but to them it has not been given.... For this reason **I speak to them in parables**, because seeing, they see not; and hearing, they hear not; neither do they understand. And in them is fulfilled the prophecy of Isaiah, which says, 'In hearing you shall hear, and in no way understand; and in seeing you shall see and in no way perceive; for the heart of this people has grown fat, and their ears are dull of hearing, and their eyes they have closed; lest they should see with their eyes, and should hear with their ears, and should understand with their hearts, and should be converted, and I should heal them' " (Matt. 13:11-15).

Up to now, only a tiny minority of all humankind has had the calling of God—and far fewer have actually come to conversion and received God's Holy Spirit. These few—this "little flock," as Christ refers to His true Church—constitute the "house of God." Peter tells us that *now*, in this life, is the time that judgment must begin at the house of God (I Pet. 4:17). Thus, when a converted person dies "in the faith" (or "in Christ") their judgment by God has already taken place. God has made the final decision that he or she is going to be in His Kingdom—and has written that person's name in the "Book of Life."

There will be some few who may have committed the "unpardonable sin"—that is, with full knowledge and understanding of the truth and the way to salvation, they have rejected God's grace and forgiveness, and have chosen not to repent and turn from the way of sin to God's way. For such—and only God knows who they are—their final judgment is complete. They await the resurrection of the wicked and their fate is the second death in the lake of fire. This lake of fire (Greek *gehenna*) is a consuming fire that totally destroys the incorrigible wicked. Jesus warned us to fear Him who can "**destroy** both soul and body" in this fire (Matt. 10:28). Malachi 4:1-3 shows that the wicked will become *ashes* under the feet of the faithful.

A *Second* Resurrection

As we've seen, the dead in Christ remain in their graves *until* He raises them up "at the last day," (Job 14:14; John 5:25; 6:39, 40, 44, 54; I Thess. 4:13-16; I Cor. 15:50-54; Matt. 24:30, 31; Rev. 20:4-6). At that time Christ will raise them to eternal life in a supernatural, spirit state—to be just like Christ Himself (I John 3:1, 2; Phil. 3:21; II Pet. 1:4; Daniel 12:3).

But what about the rest of the dead? Judgment for them has not yet occurred. When do they get their chance for salvation? In Revelation 20, verse five, John writes that the resurrection of the "dead in Christ" (which occurs at Christ's second coming) is only the "first resurrection." He adds that, "the rest of the dead lived not again until the thousand years were finished."

Thus, there is a *second* resurrection. In that same chapter, verse 12, we read, "And I saw the dead, small and great, stand before God." Here we see pictured the "second resurrection"—the resurrection of all who have ever lived and died *not* in the faith—those not having been called and brought to conversion in their first life, now coming before Christ's "white throne" of judgment.

As with most biblical subjects, the whole story is not told all in one place. Jesus mentions this general resurrection to *judgment* in several passages. For example, in Matthew 10 He says it will be "more tolerable" for the people of Sodom and Gomorrah in the "day of judgment" than those who reject the apostles' witness (verse 15). Similar statements are made elsewhere (Matt. 11:22, 24; 12:41, 42; etc.). This means people from *every generation*—ancient and modern—will be raised to life *at the same time* for judgment.

In Ezekiel 37 we have another view of the second resurrection—dealing specifically with the dead of Israel as they are brought back to physical life in the future. They are among the "rest of the dead"—the dead not in Christ—who appear before God's throne in Revelation 20:12. Remember, "the rest of the dead" means all of those not in the first resurrection—which would include the overwhelming majority of Israelites who had died throughout the ages.

Notice in Ezekiel 37 that after Israel is brought back to life, God gives them His Holy Spirit! In order to receive God's spirit, however, they must first *repent*, as Peter brings out in Acts 2:38. These newly resurrected Israelites will, apparently, be called before the "white throne" of Christ like the rest of humanity—to account for the deeds of their past. Most if not all will come to see what sinners they were, and in repentance accept Jesus Christ as their savior with forgiveness of their sins. They will be granted God's Spirit and happily live out their new physical life. (Isa. 65:20 seems to indicate that they may have up to 100 years to grow in grace and knowledge and to build spiritual character before ultimately going on into the Kingdom of God.)

Clearly then, we see "unconverted" Israel resurrected in the future. But what about "unconverted" Gentiles? Chapters 9-11 of Romans shows us that God will deal with Gentiles as He deals with Israel. Revelation 20:12 pictures *all* of the "rest of the dead" before the white throne, not just Israel. *All* bow before God and confess their sins. *All* are judged based on their works, and *all* are found guilty of sin (Rom. 3:23).

But will the guilty stand condemned? II Peter 3:9 tells us that God is not willing that any should perish (be destroyed and miss out on eternal life). After being shown their sins before the throne of God, *all* will have their *first* and *only* chance for salvation through repentance, conversion and the indwelling of the Holy Spirit. Remember, those of the second resurrection never had (in their first life) their minds opened to the truth of God by the Holy Spirit of God—and *never* had the opportunity (with a full understanding) to repent of their sins and receive God's grace.

Christ died once for *all* (I Tim. 2:6; Heb. 10:10; I Cor. 15: 22-24). Our

Lord and Savior did not go through the torture, humiliation, scourging and beating He suffered, followed by His agonizing death on the cross, only to have His grace offered to just part of the human family!

By the time this "White Throne Judgment" takes place, Satan will have been put into the lake of fire and will no longer be able to pervert the truth and deceive humanity. Without Satan's distorting influence—and with their minds now opened by the Holy Spirit—people will for the first time be able to think spiritually.

Thank God for His incredible, merciful plan! Be encouraged by the truth of the Bible concerning death and the state of the dead—rejoice in the sure knowledge that all who have ever lived will one day have their full chance for eternal life!

Does the Bible Teach the Trinity?

Millions of mainstream Christians, Catholic and Protestant, believe that God consists of three distinct persons or entities—the Father, Son and Holy Spirit—in *one* being. Put another way, God is one substance, yet three persons. Studies indicate that over 80 percent of those who believe in God hold this Trinitarian view.

It spite of this wide acceptance, the Trinity doctrine is not clearly understood by most Christians. In fact, the teaching remains largely a *mystery*, and most simply take it for granted that their pastors and church scholars are teaching the truth. The average churchgoer is not aware that even the best of scholars admit that *"the mind of man cannot fully understand the mystery of the Trinity."*[1]

As Christians, our relationship with God depends considerably on understanding His *true* nature. But how does one logically explain "three persons in one Godhead"? Our only recourse is to look to the Scriptures for the answer; indeed, our beliefs must rest solidly on the teachings of the Bible alone.

It will come as a surprise to most Christians that the word *Trinity* appears nowhere in the Bible. Where, then, does the teaching come from? Note this intriguing quote from *The Oxford Companion to the Bible*, under the article "Trinity": "Because the Trinity is such an important part of **later Christian doctrine**, it is striking that the term does not appear in the New Testament. Likewise, the developed concept of three coequal partners in the Godhead **found in later creedal formulations cannot be clearly detected within the confines of the** [New Testament] **canon.**"[2]

Pay special attention to the two phrases "**later** Christian doctrine" and "**later** creedal formulations." History shows that the original first-century church knew nothing of a "triune God." Rather, the doctrine was formulated by Greek theologians *after* the first century and was subsequently developed by later "church fathers." Notice this admission from the *New Bible Dictionary:* "The term 'Trinity' is not itself found in the Bible. It was first used by Tertullian [one of the early Catholic fathers] at the close of the 2nd century, but received wide currency [acceptance] and **formal elucidation only in the 4th and 5th centuries.**"[3]

The nature of God was hotly debated by Catholic theologians for centuries. Finally, in an effort to bring some kind of clarity and finality to the subject, church fathers met in 325 AD at the Council of Nicaea to declare an official orthodox position concerning the "divine identity." However, it wasn't until 381 AD, at the Council of Constantinople, that the "divinity" of the Holy Spirit was affirmed—making a triune Godhead.

Thus, the doctrine of the Trinity was formalized long after the Bible was completed. Over a period of several centuries, Catholic theologians ultimately sorted out what *they believed* about the Godhead—and in particular about the Holy Spirit. But as noted above, the Trinity teaching "**cannot be clearly detected within the confines of the** [New Testament] **canon**." The *Oxford* continues: "While the New Testament writers say a great deal about God, Jesus, and the Spirit of each, no New Testament writer expounds on the relationship among the three in the detail that *later Christian writers* do."[4]

Indeed, no serious scholar today claims that the Trinity teaching can be derived from the Bible. As it turns out, many of the so-called "early church fathers" were thoroughly educated in Babylonian, Egyptian, and Greek philosophy—from which they borrowed such non-biblical concepts as dualism and the immortality of the soul. As these pagan scholars came over to Christianity, they brought with them ideas and expressions that reflect Platonic philosophies. It was this pagan influence that led them to *force* a triune definition onto the Godhead. The Trinity doctrine has since been a major obstacle to the understanding that God is actually a *divine family*.

Does I John 5:7 Allow for a Trinity?

As noted, the Bible nowhere describes a triune God. But what about I John 5:7—"For there are three that bear record in heaven, the Father, the Word, and the Holy Ghost: and these three are one" (*KJV*)—does it not reveal a Trinity? As many Bible students eventually come to see, this verse is 4th-century spurious addition to the New Testament. *Peake's Commentary* says, "No respectable Greek [manuscript] contains [this passage]. Appearing first in a late 4th-century Latin text, it entered the Vulgate and finally the NT of Erasmus [and eventually the *KJV*]."[5]

Numerous Bible commentaries agree, and most modern translations omit the passage.

I John 5:6-8 should read: "This is He Who came by water and blood—Jesus the Christ; not by water only, but by water and blood. And it is the Spirit that bears witness because the Spirit is the truth. For there are three that bear witness on the earth: the Spirit, and the water, and the blood; and these three *witness* unto the one *truth*."

What this spurious passage demonstrates is that Catholic translators of the past were so zealous to find support for their preconceived belief in the Trinity that they quite literally *added* it. Remember, the Trinity teaching originated *after* the Apostle John had canonized the complete New Testament in 98-100 AD, This Catholic doctrine was not finalized until centuries later. As we will see, it is *not* a biblical concept.

Biblical Proof Disproving the Trinity Teaching

There are numerous key points that prove that the Trinity doctrine is contrary to clear biblical teaching. For example:

1) The fact that the word "trinity" is not found in the Bible casts serious doubt on the teaching.

2) The Holy Spirit is nowhere described as if it were a person. On the contrary, the Holy Spirit was "poured out" on Pentecost (Acts 2:18)—and was "poured out" upon Gentiles (Acts 10:45). A person is not "poured out." Likewise, Acts 2:2 reads: "And suddenly *there* came from heaven a sound like *the* rushing of a powerful wind, and filled the whole house...." A person does not sound like a mighty wind, and cannot fill a house. In Acts 2:3, the Holy Spirit appeared as cloven tongues—something a person cannot do.

3) Christ was conceived by the Holy Spirit (Matt. 1:18, 20). If the Holy Spirit were a person, that would make the *Holy Spirit* Christ's father, INSTEAD OF THE TRUE God the Father!

Clearly, the Holy Spirit is not a person; it is the *power* God uses to accomplish His work.

4) Jesus said, "I and My Father are one" (John 10:30; 17:21-22). He never mentioned the Holy Spirit as being one with Him and His Father.

5) Daniel, a loyal servant of God, spoke of only *two* members of the Godhead: "The **Son of man** ... came to the **Ancient of Days**, and they brought Him near before Him" (Dan. 7:13). Likewise, King David, a man after God's own heart (Acts 13:22), spoke of only *two* members of the Godhead: "The **Lord** said to my **Lord**, 'Sit at My right hand...' " (Psa. 110:1).

6) In most of his epistles, the apostle Paul gave salutations from God the Father and Christ—*but never included the Holy Spirit*. If the Holy Spirit were a person and a member of a triune Godhead, Paul would have sent greetings from the Holy Spirit as well. Moreover, in three of Paul's letters God the Father and Jesus are referred to as persons—but the Holy Spirit is never referred to as such (Col. 1:3; I Thess. 1:1; Hebrews 1:1-2).

7) In John's vision of the throne of God (Rev. 4-5), he saw only the Father and the Son. He did not see a third person designated as "God, the Holy Spirit."

But what about the fact that the New Testament often uses the term "*he*" for the Holy Spirit? The use of the personal pronoun "*he*" erroneously gives the impression that the Holy Spirit is a person. In such cases, the translators knowingly rendered the *neuter* Greek terms as the *masculine* "he"—because it fit with their preconceived idea that the Holy Spirit was one of the three "persons" of the Godhead. In all such passages, the correct translation should be *it* or *that* or *that one*.

Ultimately, Satan the devil is the force behind the Trinity teaching. Satan hates the reality of the *Family of God*. Satan's religions—including mainstream Christianity—teach a closed, triangular Trinity; the Bible teaches an *open divine family* which humans can enter.

The *Family* Nature of God

While God is eternal and composed of spirit, there is something about the fundamental nature of the Godhead that goes unnoticed by most: **God is plural in nature**—i.e., there is *more than one* Eternal Being in the Godhead. The first allusion to this fact is found in Genesis one. In creating man, God said, "Let **US** make man in **Our** image, after **Our** likeness…" (Gen. 1:26).

This language concerns *family*. Indeed, Genesis 5:3 says that Adam "begot a son *in his own likeness, after his image.*" It was after creating plants and animals to reproduce each "according to its kind" that God said, "Let Us make man in Our *image*, after Our *likeness.*" This shows that man was created according to the *God kind*. So God is essentially *reproducing Himself* through humanity!

But who are the *Us* speaking here?

Our primary clue is found in the word "God." The English word *God* is translated from the Hebrew word *Elohim*, which is a *plural* noun. This word reveals essential knowledge concerning the nature of God. Like English plural nouns, Hebrew plural nouns refer to more than one person or thing. As the plural noun "men" inherently means more than one man, *Elohim* means more than a single God Being. A number of passages in the Old Testament confirm the existence of more than one Divine Being (Gen. 1:26; 11:7; Psa. 110:1; 45:7-8; Dan. 7:13).

In fact, the Scriptures reveal that there are *two* who are *Elohim*. In the Old Testament, one *Elohim* is the God Who is called "the Most High" (Gen. 14:22) and the "Ancient of Days" (Dan. 7:13). In the New Testament He is revealed as "God the Father." The other *Elohim* in the Old Testament is the God Who is called the "LORD God" and the "Almighty God"—the God of Israel. This is the God Who later *became* Jesus, the Christ of the New Testament.

This *family nature* of the Godhead is key to understanding God's plan for mankind!

Appendix 4 Notes:

1. Harold Lindsell and Charles J. Woodbridge, *A Handbook of Christian Truth*, p. 51.

The problems in clearly explaining the Trinity are expressed in nearly every technical article or book on the subject. The *New Catholic Encyclopedia* admits: "It is difficult … in the second half of the 20th century, to offer a clear, objective, and straightforward account of the revelation, doctrinal evolution, and the theological elaboration of the mystery of the Trinity. Trinitarian discussion, Roman Catholic as well as other, *presents a somewhat unsteady silhouette*" (Vol. XIV, p. 295).

2. *The Oxford Companion to the Bible*; 1993; "Trinity"

3. *New Bible Dictionary*; 1996; "Trinity"

4. *The Oxford Companion to the Bible*; 1993; "Trinity"

5. *Peake's Bible Commentary*, p. 1038

Can the Sin of Abortion Be Forgiven?

In one form or another, *abortion* has been practiced by humankind for millennia. But only in our modern age has abortion become mainstream—made *legal* in most parts of the world. While most people are in fact morally opposed to abortion, the practice has gained a foothold in the Western world because of two key factors: 1) liberal-minded entitlement ideology (i.e., it is a woman's inherent *right* to abort a baby she does not want), and 2) the rejection of God's Word as the ultimate standard for all of life's decisions. Obviously, those who believe in the practice of abortion have no respect for the laws of God and possess no knowledge of His *purpose* for human life.

Since the practice is legal under man's law, millions of women have had abortions. For the most part, they have done so believing it to be their prerogative—that abortion is simply another aspect of a woman's overall healthcare. Shamefully, however, many have used abortion as a form of birth control—to terminate an unwanted pregnancy. Abortion proponents and providers assure women that they have absolute control over their bodies and have the legal right to have an unwanted baby forcibly removed. Often, women who have abortions do not realize that the fetus they carry is a *new life* with its own body—separate from them.

When a woman has an abortion, little does she grasp the profound consequences of her actions. Abortion inflicts devastating emotional and mental anguish, guilt and trauma that haunt her thoughts and dreams. Those who have had an abortion often relate the lonely, empty feelings they experience as they lie awake at night crying and wondering, "What have I done? What would the child have been like? Was it a boy or a girl?" It is at that moment, perhaps, that they begin to sense the magnitude of their choice.

Instead of nurturing and sustaining the new life in her body, she has, through abortion, *taken a life*— the most helpless of all! Had she only realized that the baby was not a "mass of disposable cells"—*but a new human life*—she might have made a different decision.

New Human Life Begins at Conception

It is a scientific fact that *at conception* the new human life fully possesses, from its father and mother, all the genes and chromosomes needed to become a complete human being. As the Bible shows, it is also *at conception* that one receives the *spirit of man* from God. Now, all the baby needs is time to grow and develop in the womb and be born. Thus, at every stage of life, from conception to death, every human being is made in the image and likeness of God.

Accordingly, God has ordained that the *deliberate* taking of a human life—regardless of age—is murder. It is the breaking of God's Sixth Commandment, "You shall not murder!" And, the violation of God's laws is *sin*—for "sin is the transgression of the law" (I John 3:4; *KJV*).

Regardless of the circumstances or motivation for having an abortion, it is the deliberate termination of a human life. Thus, God reckons it as sin!

Can the Sin of Abortion Be Forgiven?

The answer is a resounding *yes!* But such forgiveness can only be obtained upon deep, heartfelt *repentance*. Jesus declared, "**[E]very sin and blasphemy shall be forgiven to men** except the blasphemy against the *Holy* Spirit; *that* shall not be forgiven to men. And whoever speaks a word against the Son of man, it shall be forgiven him; but whoever speaks against the Holy Spirit, it shall not be forgiven him, neither in this age nor in the coming *age*" (Matt. 12:31-32).[1]

The apostle John writes, "**If we confess our own sins** [directly to God—see Psalm 51], **He is faithful and righteous, to forgive us our sins**, and to cleanse us from all unrighteousness" (I John 1:9).

Jesus also warned that, after being forgiven of our sins, we are to go and sin no more (John 5:14; 8:11). Rather, we are to be baptized by full immersion in water for the complete remission of sins, as Peter proclaimed: "Repent and be baptized each one of you in the name of Jesus Christ for *the* remission of sins, and you yourselves shall receive the gift of the Holy Spirit" (Acts 2:38). We are then to walk in newness of life—in God's way of life.

Since human life begins at *conception*, what happens if the baby is killed by abortion? Will it live again? If so, how? The answer is this: At conception, every new human life has *everything* it will need to become a complete person. But its life was cut short by abortion. However, at conception, its entire genetic code was "imprinted" on the "spirit of man" it received from God. When the baby died, this "spirit" returned to God (see Eccl. 12:7). God *maintains* this "spirit of man," using it to *restore to life* all who are in the second resurrection—the time when *all* who never received an opportunity for eternal life during their first physical life will be raised from the dead to a second physical life. This includes *all unborn children* who were aborted, died in the womb, or were miscarried. Undoubtedly, they will be raised as full term newborn infants. In all likelihood, where possible, these infants will be given to their own mothers and fathers.

At this time, the *final phase* of the "Mystery of God" will begin!

For further details on the second resurrection, please see Appendix 3, *What Happens After Death?*

Appendix 5 Note:

1. The "unpardonable sin"—blasphemy against the Holy Spirit—is when a person *chooses* to be unrepentant, demonstrating an unmistakable hatred of God, His laws, and His rule in one's life. To commit the "unpardonable sin," an individual would be adamant and hardhearted in their refusal to repent of their sins. Thus, he or she *rejects* God the Father and the power of the Holy Spirit with malice and forethought.

Appendix Six

What Does it Mean to Be "Born Again" or "Born of God"?

According to mainstream Christianity, one is "born again" when he or she has "received Christ" and been "saved"—typically at baptism. Thus, being "born again" is seen as a *religious experience*. Yet most Christians have great difficulty explaining from Scripture what it means to be "born again" or "born of God."[1] Indeed, there is great confusion on this subject. The Bible, however, is quite straightforward on the topic.

In John 3:1-12, Jesus taught that to be "born again" literally means to be "born of the Spirit"—to *become* a spirit being. As we will see, other passages show that this "new birth" to spirit life will take place at the first resurrection when Christ returns. Thus, Jesus is the only one who has been "born again"—as He is the *firstborn from the dead*. No one else has yet been resurrected from the dead to eternal life—no one else has been "born again."

The Pagan Origin of the Popular "Born Again" Doctrine

It may come as a surprise to many that the idea of a "second birth" *as a religious experience* is not unique to Christianity. In fact, the concept is quite ancient. In his epochal book *The Two Babylons*, Alexander Hislop demonstrates that pagan religions, which had their roots in ancient Babylon, had a belief and practice of being "born again" or "twice born." For example, Hislop wrote: "The Brahmins make it their distinguishing boast that they are 'twice-born' men, and that, as such, they are sure of eternal happiness. Now, the same was the case in [ancient] Babylon, and there **the new birth was conferred by baptism**" (p. 132, emphasis added). Note that the pagan teaching of being "born again" or "twice born" had nothing to do with being raised from the dead, and that it was linked to the rite of *baptism*.

But how did this false teaching find its way into nominal Christianity?

Jesus repeatedly warned His followers about false messiahs, false apostles, and false teachers who would, if possible, deceive the very elect (Matt. 24:5, 11, 15, 24; see parallel accounts in Mark and Luke). The apostles likewise warned believers to be on guard against false apostles and teachers (II Cor. 4:11; I and II Timothy; Titus 1; II Pet. 2; I, II and III John; Jude; Rev. 2, 3, 13 and 17). The New Testament is replete with warnings about false apostles and teachers who would come in "sheep's clothing" but would inwardly be "ravening wolves," seeking to pervert and destroy the truth.

The apostle Paul warned the Thessalonians in 51 AD that an apostate religious system, which he called the "mystery of lawlessness," was beginning to penetrate the Church (II Thess. 2:1-12). He warned, "Do not let anyone deceive you by any means because *that day* [of Christ's return] *will not* come unless **the apostasy shall come first**, and the man of sin [the final anti-Christ] shall be revealed.... **For the mystery of lawlessness is already working**" (verses 2, 7).

Over time, this "mystery religion," modeled after the ancient Babylonian "mysteries," has developed into a great apostate "Christianity"—which Christ has identified in Scripture as "**Babylon the Great, the mother of the harlots and of the abominations of the earth**" (Rev. 17:5). The early leaders of this religious system established numerous false teachings, among them the doctrine that one is "born again" at conversion—or, in Protestant-speak, when one has "accepted Jesus." Just as in ancient Babylon, this "new birth" is associated with baptism, but has nothing to do with being raised from the dead to spirit life.

Early Latin "church fathers" adopted the Babylonian idea that one is "born again" through baptism. *Justin Martyr*, for example, taught that converts to Christianity are to be "led ... to a place where there is **water**; and **there they are reborn** in the same kind of rebirth in which we ourselves were reborn" (*The First Apology*, 61). *Irenaeus* taught that Christians "are made clean, by means of the **sacred water** and the invocation of the Lord, from [their] old transgressions, being spiritually **regenerated as new-born babes**..." (*Fragment*, 34). Likewise, *Clement* wrote that, in this present life, Christians "are **regenerated** and **born again of water**" (*Recognitions, 6:9*). These statements reveal that the early "church fathers" believed that being "born again" was a *religious experience* tied to the rite of baptism.

A contributing factor that has obscured the true meaning of the phrase "born again" is the mistranslation of John 3:5 in the *Latin Vulgate*. Originally translated by Jerome in 383 AD, the *Vulgate* inserts the word "again" into verse five, making it read "born **again** of water." Yet no Greek manuscript includes the word "again" in the passage. By contrast, Erasmus' Latin translation from the Greek correctly renders the verse as simply "born of water."

Is probable that the Latin church leaders—such as those quoted above—were influenced by an early, pre-*Vulgate* translation of the Scriptures with a corrupt rendering of John 3:5. At the very least, Jerome's translation perpetuated the false "born again" teaching with its corruption of John 3:5. The faulty rendering has remained a part of the *Latin Vulgate* and is the basis of the Catholic "sacrament of baptism"—typically given to infants or children.

Biblical scholar William Tyndale, the first to translate the New Testament from the Greek into English, translated John 3:3, 5 correctly. However, in other writings he taught that when one is converted and receives the Holy Spirit, one has been "born again." It is likely that Tyndale's theology contributed to the Protestant "born again" teaching.

The True Meaning of "Born Again"

In order to fully comprehend the scriptural meaning of when one is "born again," Jesus' teachings in John 3:1-12 must be examined. The context of these verses proves that being "born again" does *not* mean a conversion or baptismal experience. Rather, it means a literal *transformation from flesh to spirit*: "Now there was a man of the Pharisees, Nicodemus by name, a ruler of the Jews. He came to Jesus by night and said to Him, 'Rabbi, we know that You are a teacher *Who* has come from God; because no one is able to do the miracles that You are doing, unless God is with him.'

"Jesus answered and said to him, 'Truly, truly I say to you, **unless anyone is born again**, he cannot see the kingdom of God.' Nicodemus said to Him, 'How can a man who is old be born? Can he enter his mother's womb a second time and be born?' Jesus answered, 'Truly, truly I say to you, **unless anyone has been born of water and of Spirit**, he cannot enter the kingdom of God. That which has been **born of the flesh is flesh**; and that which has been **born of the Spirit is spirit**. Do not be amazed that I said to you, "It is necessary for you to be born again." **The wind blows where it will**, and you hear its sound, but you do not know *the place* from which it comes and *the place* to which it goes; so *also* **is everyone who has been born of the Spirit**.'

"Nicodemus answered and said to Him, 'How can these things be?' Jesus answered and said to him, 'You are a teacher of Israel, and you do not know these things? Truly, truly I say to you, We speak that which We know, and We testify of that which We have seen; but you do not receive Our testimony. If I have told you earthly things, and you do not believe, how will you believe if I tell you heavenly things?' " (John 3:1-12).

It is clear that Jesus was not talking about a conversion or baptismal experience in this dialogue. Rather, he was comparing one's physical birth—a fleshly existence—to that of being "born anew" or "born again"—to an actual spiritual existence. Jesus describes two births: one of water and one of the spirit—"unless anyone has been **born of water** and **of Spirit**" (John 3:5). Jesus then contrasts a birth of the flesh with a birth of the Spirit: "That which has been **born of the flesh is flesh**; and that which has been **born of the Spirit is spirit**" (verse 6).

When a human being is born, he or she is *born of flesh*—a physical being. Further, every human being has been "born of water" from the womb—referring to the amniotic fluid of human birth. One who has been *born of water* (via the womb) **has been born of the flesh—and** *is* **flesh** (John 3:5-6).

But Nicodemus missed the point when Jesus referred to a new or second birth of the Spirit—**"unless anyone has been born ... of Spirit."** What kind of *existence* does one have who has been "born of the Spirit"? Jesus answered that question when He said "that which has been **born of the Spirit is spirit**." Jesus clearly meant that anyone who has been born of the Spirit is, in fact, **a spirit being**. The new, spiritual birth means that one who has been "born again" *is* a spirit being, no longer composed of human flesh. Since one who has been "born of the flesh is flesh," it follows, as Jesus said, that one who has been "born of the Spirit is spirit" (John 3:6).

Every human is limited by fleshly existence and physical environment. However, as a spirit being, one is not bound by the flesh or limited by the physical realm. Jesus stated that one who has been "born of the Spirit" cannot necessarily be seen, just as the wind cannot be seen: **"The wind blows where it wills**, and you hear its sound, but you do not know *the place* from which it comes and *the place* to which it goes; **so** *also* **is everyone who has been born of the Spirit"** (verse 8). Therefore, one who has been "born again"—"born of the Spirit"—must be invisible to the human eye, having the ability to come and go as the wind. That is hardly the case of one who has been baptized and converted—for he or she is *still* in the flesh and is limited by the flesh, absolutely visible and subject to death.

Jesus also said that a fleshly human being "cannot see" or "enter into" the Kingdom of God (John 3:3, 5). Paul reiterated this when he emphatically stated: "Now this I say, brethren, that flesh and blood cannot inherit *the* kingdom of God" (I Cor. 15:50).

When Is One Actually Born Again?

When, then, is one literally "born again" or "born anew"? It is through the birth, life, death, and resurrection of Christ that the New Testament reveals *when* a person is "born again." Matthew wrote that Jesus was the "firstborn" of the virgin Mary (Matt. 1:25). Jesus' human birth was by water. He was flesh (I John 4:1-2), as any other human being, but He was "God manifested in *the* flesh" (I Tim. 3:16).

When Jesus was resurrected from the dead *as a spirit being*, He became, in Paul's words, the **"firstborn from among the dead"** (Col. 1:18). John verified this when he wrote that Jesus was the **"firstborn from the** dead" (Rev. 1:5). Therefore, Jesus was "born again"—"born of the Spirit"—at the time He was *resurrected*. It was exactly as He had told Nicodemus, "That which has been born of the Spirit **is spirit**."

As a spirit being, Jesus was not limited by the physical realm. In fact, He walked through doors and walls, suddenly appearing to the apostles and disciples (Luke 24:33-43). Though spirit, Jesus was able to manifest Himself as a man, with the appearance of flesh and bone.

Christ Is the Firstborn Among Many

Not only is Jesus the firstborn from the dead, He is also the "**firstborn** among many brethren" (Rom. 8:29). If Jesus is the *firstborn*, this means there are others who are yet to be "born again." The true body of believers is called the "church of the firstborn," as Paul wrote: "But you have come to Mount Sion, and to *the* city of *the* living God, heavenly Jerusalem; and to an innumerable company of angels; *to the* joyous festival gathering; and to *the* **church of *the* firstborn**, registered *in the book of life* in heaven; and to God, *the* Judge of all" (Heb. 12:22-23). It is called the "church of the firstborn" because believers will be "born again"—"born of the Spirit"—in the first resurrection when Jesus returns (Rev. 20:4-6).

The Bible reveals that at the resurrection believers will be "born again" of the Spirit and receive a glorious spirit body, shining as the sun. Paul explains: "It [the body] is sown [in death] **a natural body** [that which has been born of the flesh *is flesh*]; it is raised [in the first resurrection] **a spiritual body** [that which has been born of the spirit *is spirit*]. **There is a natural body**, and **there is a spiritual body**; accordingly, it is written, 'The first man, Adam, became a living soul; the last Adam *became* an ever-living Spirit.' However, the spiritual *was* not first, but the natural—then the spiritual.

"The first man *is* of the earth—made of dust. The second man *is* the Lord from heaven. As *is* the one made of dust, so also *are all* those who are made of dust; and as *is* the heavenly *one*, so also *are all* those who are heavenly. And as we have borne the image of the *one* made of dust, **we shall also bear the image of the heavenly *one*** [at the resurrection].

"Now this I say, brethren, that **flesh and blood cannot inherit *the* kingdom of God**, nor does corruption inherit incorruption. Behold, I show you a mystery: we shall not all fall asleep, but **we shall all be changed** [born again of the Spirit], in an instant, in *the* twinkling of an eye, at the last trumpet; for *the* trumpet shall sound, and **the dead shall be raised incorruptible**, and **we shall be changed**. For this corruptible must put on incorruptibility, and this mortal must put on immortality. Now when this **corruptible**

shall have put on incorruptibility, and this **mortal shall have put on im-mortality**, then shall come to pass the saying that is written: 'Death is swallowed up in victory' " (I Cor. 15:44-55; also see I Thess. 4:14-18).

In summary, the scriptural evidence clearly reveals that one is not "born again" or "born of the Spirit" until the resurrection at the return of Christ. Being "born again" has nothing directly to do with baptism or conversion. When one has been "born again," he or she will be a spirit being—composed of spirit. This is the true meaning of "born again."

For a full discussion of being "born again," please request our free booklet *What Do You Mean—Born Again and Born of God?*

Appendix 6 Notes:

1. Contributing to the confusion on this subject is the "born of God" passage in I John 3:9—a verse that has been grossly mistranslated. Unfortunately, this mistranslation has led many to mistakenly assume that Christians who are "born of God" (or "born again") *cannot sin*. But as we have seen, no Christian has yet been "born again" or "born of God." Moreover, the idea that Christians are *immune* from sinning is obviously false.

The *KJV* reads: "Whosoever is **born** of God **doth not commit sin**; for his seed remaineth in him: and **he cannot sin**, because he is **born** of God." As translated, this verse contradicts other verses in I John, as well as the rest of the New Testament.

Contrary to this incorrect translation, John wrote that even Christians who have the Holy Spirit *do indeed sin* at times—and that they need to confess their sins for forgiveness (I John 1:7-10; 2:1-2). Frankly, it would be completely incongruous for John to write the passages above about how converted believers *do* sometimes sin and, at the same time, write in I John 3:9 that one who has been "born of God" (or "born again") "does not commit sin"—and that such a person "cannot sin." Since the Scriptures do not contradict one another, what is the solution?

It is apparent that I John 3 cannot be referring to those "born again" to spirit existence by a resurrection; as shown above, *only* Jesus has been "born again" as spirit by being resurrected from the dead. No one else has been or will be "born again" by a resurrection until Christ's return. Thus, I John 3:9 can *only* apply to Christians *still alive*.

The problem with this passage comes from two mistranslated words or phrases. First, the word "born" is translated from the Greek verb *gennao*. In the *KJV*, *gennao* has been translated as "beget, begat" or "begotten" 55 times; as "born" 37 times; and as "conceive, bear, brought forth, deliver, or gender" 4 times. The context determines whether *gennao* should be translated "begotten" or "born" (Wigram, *Englishman's Greek Concordance of the New Testament*).

With this understanding, the first part of I John 3:9 can be corrected by simply translating *gennao* as "begotten" instead of "born." As a result, the correct rendering should read: "Everyone **who has been begotten** by God...."

The second phrase in I John 3:9 that has not been accurately translated in the *KJV* is "doth not commit sin." There is no question that a converted person does, at times, commit sin; but upon true repentance, through the grace of God and by the blood of Christ, those sins can be forgiven. The key to understanding this phrase is an accurate translation of the Greek verb *poiei*, translated "commit." As used in verse 9, *poiei* is a third person, singular, present tense form of the verb *poieo*, which means: "*to do*, generally, i.e., habitually, *to perform, to execute, to exercise, **to practice**, i.e., to pursue a course of action, to be active, to work...*" (Berry, *Greek-English Lexicon of the New Testament*, p. 81).

The context of John's epistle is not about a Christian's inability to commit sin. Therefore, *poiei* in this context means **habitually practicing sin**. When *poiei* in verse 9 is rendered "does not *practice* sin," the contradiction created by the *KJV* is removed. The correct translation of this portion of verse 9 reads: "**Everyone who has been begotten by God does not practice sin.**"

This is a true statement and conveys the original meaning of the Greek. Furthermore, this meaning of *poiei* is retained in the second part of verse 9 with reference to "cannot sin," which should read, "cannot *practice* sin." Consequently, the entire verse correctly translated should read: "Everyone who has been begotten by God does not practice sin because His seed *of begettal* is dwelling within him, and he is not able to *practice* sin because he has been begotten by God." This rendering harmonizes with the rest of John's epistle (and the entire New Testament) and removes all contradictions.

One of the reasons for confusion on this subject is that many fail to understand that conversion is an *ongoing process*. In one sense, a person is "converted" when they have repented, been baptized for the remission of their sins, and received the Holy Spirit (by which they are actually *begotten*). In another sense, however, their conversion has only *just begun*. As a process of change and growth, conversion takes place over one's lifetime. Thus, sin still sometime occurs—but not as a way of life or practice. Only at the end of that period of growth, change, and overcoming is the Christian finally "born again" at the resurrection into the spirit Family of God.

Christian Biblical Church of God Offices:

United States
Post Office Box 1442
Hollister, California 95024-1442

Canada
Post Office Box 125
Brockville, Ontario
K6V 5V2 Canada

Australia
GPO 1574
Sydney 2001
Australia

United Kingdom
Post Office Box 8224
Witham CM8 1WZ
United Kingdom

New Zealand
Post Office Box 73
Pokeno 2473
New Zealand

Republic of South Africa
Post Office Box 494
Frankfort 9830
Rep. of South Africa

Iglesia de Dios Cristiana y Bíblica
www.iglesiadedioscristianaybiblica.org
Post Office Box 831241
San Antonio, Texas 78283

www.cbcg.org
www.churchathome.org
www.theoriginalbiblerestored.org
www.afaithfulversion.org